HOME OFFICE RESEARCH STUDY NO. 90

Police-Public Encounters

by Peter Southgate
with the assistance of
Paul Ekblom

A HOME OFFICE
RESEARCH AND PLANNING
UNIT REPORT

LONDON: HER MAJESTY'S STATIONERY OFFICE

ISBN 0 11 340834 X

HOME OFFICE RESEARCH STUDIES

'Home Office Research Studies' comprise reports on research undertaken in the Home Office to assist in the exercise of its administrative functions, and for the information of the judicature, the services for which the Home Secretary has responsibility (direct or indirect) and the general public.

On the last pages of this report are listed titles already published in this series, in the preceding series *Studies in the Causes of Delinquency and the Treatment of Offenders*, and in the series of *Research and Planning Unit Papers*.

Her Majesty's Stationery Office

Standing order service

Placing a standing order with HMSO BOOKS enables a customer to receive other titles in this series automatically as published.

This saves time, trouble and expense of placing individual orders and avoids the problem of knowing when to do so.

For details please write to HMSO BOOKS (PC13A/1), Publications Centre, PO Box 276, London SW8 5DT and quoting reference X25.08.07.

The standing order service also enables customers to receive automatically as published all material of their choice which additionally saves extensive catalogue research. The scope and selectivity of the service has been extended by new techniques, and there are more than 3,500 classifications to choose from. A special leaflet describing the service in detail may be obtained on request.

Foreword

In its 1983 report on Community and Race Relations Training for the Police the Police Training Council made various recommendations for the future. One of these was that such training must make use of a wide variety of methods, including case studies and role playing scenarios. The report said that 'If role playing scenarios are to be of real help to individual officers they will need to be based on detailed and objective observational studies of actual events. The nature of these encounters and the skills required to deal successfully with them need to be analysed and documented. . .'

A Research and Planning Unit project has addressed this proposal by gathering data on police-public street encounters. Observational methods were used by a team of field workers who accompanied uniformed patrol officers in three different cities: London, Birmingham and Bristol. Their observations were brought together in both written form and in discussion with RPU researchers and serving police officers. The result is an account of the kinds of human relations problems which can arise when police officers and members of the public come into contact with each other, and as these encounters develop.

Appended to the report are a selection of case studies, comprising descriptions of, and dialogue from, a number of the encounters witnessed. It is hoped that these will prove useful to police trainers as classroom material.

The conclusion to the report considers the implications of the data for police-public relations and for police training. It notes that, although the vast majority of encounters proceed in a polite and friendly manner, there are a few examples of very bad practice and a great many more where there is room for improvement. Some of this improvement can come through better training, while some of it requires changes in the organisation and its procedures. Training should not hope to provide all the answers for every situation, but it should try to make officers more flexible and creative in their problem solving, and help them recognise that they must deal effectively with human relations problems as well as legal ones.

MARY TUCK
Head of the Research and Planning Unit

May 1986

Acknowledgements

A number of people contributed ideas and practical help at various stages of this project. But thanks should go first to my colleague Paul Ekblom who provided valuable ideas, insights and comments at all stages of the work, particularly in relation to the development and application of the group discussion technique used during the regular meetings with the observer team.

Within the police service, I am most grateful for the help and cooperation received from the Metropolitan Police, Avon and Somerset Constabulary and West Midlands Police, within whose areas the main observational work took place. In the developmental stages of the work help was also received from the Metropolitan Police and from the Hertfordshire and Hampshire Constabularies.

Valuable comments were received at various stages from colleagues in the Research and Planning Unit and from researchers elsewhere, from individual police officers, and from staff at the Metropolitan Police Training School at Hendon and the Centre for the Study of Community and Race Relations at Brunel University.

This was not a project for which the data could easily have been gathered single-handedly, and the efforts and insights of the observer team were central to its success. This team comprised Philip Crowdy, Tim Grosvenor, John Habershon, Gregory Lyne, Robin McGregor, Victoria de la Torre and Ruth Trenbirth. Tim Grosvenor and John Habershon of Steer, Davies and Gleave Ltd also played an important role in managing field staff and processing data, and Victoria de la Torre helped to prepare case study material.

PETER SOUTHGATE

Contents

		Page
Foreword		iii
Acknowledgements		iv
Chapter 1	**Introduction**	1
Chapter 2	**Research methods**	7
Chapter 3	**Expectations**	11
Chapter 4	**Entering the encounter**	17
Chapter 5	**Processing the encounter**	25
Chapter 6	**Leaving the encounter**	47
Chapter 7	**Conclusions**	53
Appendix	**— I Case studies**	59
	— II Methodology	129
References		141

1 Introduction

In its report on Community and Race Relations Training for the Police (Home Office, 1983) the Police Training Council made various recommendations for the future. One of these was that racism awareness training should form part of the training of all police officers (Southgate, 1984; Bull, 1985). Another was that community and race relations training must make use of a wide variety of methods, including case studies and role playing scenarios. The report said that "If role playing scenarios are to be of real help to individual officers they will need to be based on detailed and objective observational studies of actual events. The nature of these encounters and the skills required to deal successfully with them need to be analysed and documented....We believe that such research will be essential to underpin future skills training and we recommend that it is carried out without delay." The following report describes a study undertaken by the Home Office Research and Planning Unit in response to this recommendation of the Working Party, and to the now growing interest from the police service in the development of this aspect of policing skills. In his Report for the Year 1984, for example, the Metropolitan Police Commissioner refers to "the importance of the human dimension of policing skills in training (Home Office, 1985)."

It is widely felt that police training has concentrated in the past on procedural and legal aspects of the job, at the expense of the human relations side of policing. While the former aspects are obviously vital, modern policing brings the officer into contact with a wide range of people in a wide range of circumstances (Southgate and Ekblom, 1984), many of which do not fit neatly into the kinds of categories implied by earlier recruit training syllabuses. In the extreme, such a lack of appropriate training can contribute to serious conflict between police and some sections of the public, as happened in the riots of recent years. But at a less dramatic level there are many points of contact between police and public where trouble can arise, even though it may not escalate into a riot; for example, traffic stops, domestic disputes or visits to crime victims. Almost any contact can, in principle, go wrong at some point if one party reacts inappropriately towards the other, or is perceived as doing so. As Goffman (1971), Argyle (1969) and others have shown, the rules of social interaction are complex and varied. Some are generally understood and respected while others are not; many are specific to certain cultures; many are specific to particular role or status relationships. In policing, for example, a common expectation is that the office of constable should attract a certain degree of deference from those who have dealings with the holder of that office. If the relationship between police officer and citizen is seen in terms of these expectations then problems can arise where one party does not defer to the other in the expected manner (Sykes and Clark, 1975).

1

One reason for a mismatch between the realities of policing and the emphasis of training may be that not enough effort has been made to draw into training the experience of the men and women on the beat. There is no clear reason why this is so; the assumption has, perhaps, tended to be that because police trainers are drawn from the ranks they will bring with them sufficient street wisdom to pass on to their students. This wisdom is certainly there, but it is not always enough, because it is only one person's interpretation of their own experiences. Trainers may assume that the experience of others is the same as theirs, but this may not be so; also, they may fail to pass on the most useful or appropriate lessons from their own experience. What is certainly true is that the way one person copes with a particular situation can be different in important ways from the way another person handles it, so that it is important for training to be based upon information representing a wide range of policing experience. It is in this respect that research of the kind reported here can be valuable. It brings together the experiences of police officers of different kinds working in different places, and draws from this lessons which are in some cases general ones and in other cases of relevance to very specific situations, some of which can occur frequently in day to day uniformed patrol work. Throughout the study, the aim has been to focus upon what is problematic; that is, those situations which are sufficiently complex, ambiguous or otherwise in doubt that the way to resolve them cannot be specified and learned in a cut and dried way.

Previous research

A great deal is already known about encounters between police and public, derived from sample surveys among the public, studies of police workloads, observational studies and experimental or quasi-experimental research. One point to emerge very clearly from such work is that only a minority of calls upon the police — perhaps little more than one third — are concerned with crime, with the rest consisting of 'service' or public order matters (Punch and Naylor, 1973; Hough, 1980; Jones, 1983). This contrasts with the typical police officer's view of his role which tends to emphasise the pursuit of law breakers (Manning, 1977; Holdaway, 1977; Reiner, 1978; Smith and Gray, 1983).

One important issue is the extent to which contacts involve hostility, ill feeling or conflict between police and public. Survey evidence suggests that overall, only a minority are actually dissatisfied with the police (NOP, 1981: Southgate and Ekblom, 1984) and evidence from observational studies shows that even in high crime areas such as New York City conflict between police and public is actually quite uncommon (Sichel et al., 1978). Nevertheless, just because the majority expresses satisfaction or has friendly contacts with the police, it must not be assumed that no problem exists. Analysis of British Crime Survey data (Southgate and Ekblom, 1984) suggested that about one person in six had experienced some contact with the police in the previous year which was 'adversarial', in that the person was being treated as a suspected offender. For one person in seventeen this was their only police contact in that year. The PSI study produced a similar finding, with one encounter in seven involving the respondent as an offender or suspect (Smith and Gray, 1983), and it is clear from these and other studies (eg Kinsey, 1985) that critical feelings towards the police are very common among those who have encountered them in this way, by being stopped in the street on foot or in a vehicle.

A recent British observational study of road users and the police examined encounters between traffic police and drivers they stopped (Dix and Layzell, 1983). This brought out very clearly the problematic nature of these contacts and the interaction problems which may arise in the particular circumstances of the traffic stop. It made some limited comments on the training implications, but its conclusions were inevitably rather tentative because of the small numbers of encounters observed.

Probably the most widely known recent British observational study of the police has been that conducted by the Policy Studies Institute in the Metropolitan Police. This was part of a broad programme of research by PSI whose purpose was to provide "... a new understanding ... of relations between the police and people in London, and of policing policy, practice and organisation" (Smith and Gray, 1983). The observational part of the study took place over a two-year period and looked at a wide range of police work, and provided many insights into the informal norms and behaviour of uniformed patrol and CID officers.

In producing data which might be useful in understanding police-public encounters, one of the most difficult aspects is to capture their essence as processes rather than as discrete events. Few studies have succeeded fully in doing this. Bayley and Bittner (1985) suggest a classification system which goes some way in this direction. They propose a division of the encounter into three stages: contact, processing and exit with, at each stage, a certain number of tactical choices which are open to the police officer. They choose as illustrations traffic stops and domestic disputes on the grounds that police cite these as two of the most problematic (in the sense that they contain many points of doubt and uncertainty) which they have to deal with though, in principle at least, the options for any type of encounter might be distinguished in this way. In traffic stops, for example, they see ten possible actions at the first contact stage, seven while processing the incident, and eleven at the exit stage. The following are some examples. At contact: leave the driver in the car, order him out, ask for documents, ask if the driver knew why he was stopped. At processing: give a breath test, make a body search, search the vehicle. At exit: release car and driver, release with a warning, arrest driver, impound the car. Equivalent actions are described for domestic disturbances.

There does seem to be some overlap between the three stages. Thus, for example, where he is dealing with more than one person, the officer may not always perform 'exit' actions at the end and 'processing' actions in the middle. However, the choice of actions to be taken probably remains the same, and this three-stage framework for description and analysis certainly provides a useful structure for both the researcher and the trainer.

One of the most detailed large scale observational studies of police-public encounters was done by Sykes and colleagues from the early 1970s onwards in the United States. (Sykes and Clark, 1975; Sykes and Brent, 1983). Encounters were observed and documented using electronic recording devices which — after lengthy training and practice — allowed each utterance by officers and citizens to be coded and recorded directly on to tape.

Methodically, the Sykes and Brent study would have been impossible to replicate in the time available for the present research. It was primarily a piece of basic research set first within a linguistic research tradition and contributing at least as much to that field of knowledge as to any understanding of policing. It provides a valuable example and source of ideas, though it is certainly quite sobering in some of its conclusions and about our understanding of encounters. The authors feel, for example, that the effects of personal, demographic or situational variables upon encounters are actually extremely difficult to predict because they may be neutralised or amplified by events during the course of the encounter itself. They also conclude that it would probably not be sensible or even possible at the moment to look for one theory of police-civilian interaction; the best that can be achieved being a theory of some particular aspect of police behaviour such as brutality, report-taking, or giving a traffic ticket (Sykes and Brent, 1983).

The Sykes and Brent study was concerned particularly with verbal interaction, because this is the most common way in which police-public encounters are handled. But on many occasions it is equally vital to take account of non-verbal communication. A laboratory study by Garratt et al. (1981) demonstrates most clearly the significance of this in the context of inter-ethnic police-public encounters. Black subjects were exposed to a short routine interview with white police officers. These officers were first trained to conduct the interviews using both an 'anglo' and a 'black' style, the differences relating to how the officer entered a room, looked at the subject, moved about and positioned himself in relation to him. The subjects were each interviewed in the two different ways and then completed a questionnaire which asked them a series of questions about the two officers. The black subjects consistently showed a preference for the officer who conducted the interview with them using the 'black' style. As the authors themselves admit there are many qualifications to be put upon these results, not least that there was no comparative element using white subjects. But results such as this do tend to suggest both (a) the importance of culture-specific body language in interactions and (b) the potential for affecting the quality of police-public contacts through training officers to behave in certain ways in certain situations. The acceptance of these principles is implied in the various programmes in intercultural training which are now used by governments, military forces, and business organisations sending staff to work in unfamiliar cultures (eg Landis and Brislin, 1983).

Ethnic minorities

One issue in designing this study was, indeed, the question of how far it should focus specifically upon contacts between police and ethnic minorities; the need for better relationships between police and ethnic minorities was, of course, a central concern of the Working Party which recommended the study. But the question as to whether the police should behave in particular ways when speaking to minority groups is a complex and emotive one and the Working Party noted two main points of view. On the one hand, it believed that good community relations and good race relations shared common requirements and needed similar skills. It was also concerned that treating race relations training separately "...might inadvertently perpetuate the notion that our minority ethnic communities constitute simply another 'problem' group for the police". On the other hand, it was argued that "...racial and cultural differences can introduce complexities of a special nature and order into encounters..." and that race relations should not be dealt with simply as a species of human relations (Home Office, 1983).

About one in seven of the encounters in the present study involved ethnic minority people. In some cases this seemed to have some bearing upon what went on, but mostly there was little to distinguish these encounters from the majority of those witnessed, as far as either subject matter, dialogue or behaviour were concerned. The selection of the case studies appended to this report has, in fact, been weighted towards these encounters to reflect the particular interest in them. But most of the discussion in the report is more broadly focused, for there seems little point in advising police officers how to relate to ethnic minorities unless these skills are founded upon a wider competence in dealing successfully with the public as a whole.

Drawing out training implications

The term 'training' can refer to all the many ways in which a person learns how to do a given job, and this clearly encompasses more than simply what takes place in the classroom. It would, indeed, be very easy to broaden the definition to take in all aspects of the socialisation of recruits into the world of policing; although the temptation to do this has largely been resisted, this has not always been possible.

The data provide evidence as to how aware officers were of the human relations problems they faced, of the skills they possessed for dealing with them, and of the negative and positive lessons to be learnt. The report expresses some views as to what training needs are, but its primary purpose is to present issues and examples, showing as much as possible about the way problems arise and the ways in which police officers cope with them.

Problems described in this report are not intended to be an exhaustive list of what police officers do. No matter how many hours of police-public contact might be observed, it is unlikely that examples would have been seen of every single incident or problem which a uniformed constable is likely to encounter. The study set out to observe contacts in areas which were busy urban areas and seemed likely to produce some of the more difficult policing situations. Policing conditions do, of course, vary significantly from one force to another, and from one division to another within a force. The usual reservation might be made, therefore, that the results are not fully generalisable beyond the police subdivisions or forces involved in the study. This will be true in any such study, but it is unlikely that all elements of a situation would differ at once from one place to another; many common elements persist in patterns of human behaviour even though environments, legal constraints or social traditions may vary. The study did not set out to compare one police force with another, and it was clear in any case that the experiences of English police officers were not vastly different whether they took place in London, Birmingham or Bristol; comparison with other research studies also supports this view.

The results presented often show the police in a critical light. This does not mean that most of the things they did were wrong; indeed, some of the examples quoted are examples of very good practice. The only purpose in emphasising problems is in hoping that they will provide a basis from which police trainers can start with their students in exploring alternative and better tactics.

The rest of this report contains three main elements. First, there is a description of the research methods (summarised in the main text and discussed in detail in an appendix) and an overview of the encounters witnessed. Second, there are discussions of the various human relations problems which arose during the course of the encounters. Third, there are conclusions and suggestions as to how training for this aspect of policing may best be advanced. Finally, appended to the report is a selection of case studies. The intention is not for the case studies to illustrate every point in the text, because this would make for an overly long appendix. Some points are illustrated in this way, but an equally important function is to show more generally how police and public actually talk to each other, and a few of the issues they talk about. No doubt they will also raise new issues, and this will be especially valuable to police trainers in the classroom.

2 Research methods

This chapter presents a very brief account of the methods used to gather and analyse the data. A fuller description is appended to the report for the benefit of those with a particular interest in methodology or who may wish to replicate or modify the methods used for their own purposes.

Fieldwork

Following a month of pre-testing and piloting work, the main fieldwork was conducted from two police stations each in the Metropolitan Police, West Midlands Police and Avon and Somerset Constabulary areas. The intention was to focus the study on urban areas where policing conditions would be busy and challenging, and where a fair proportion of encounters might involve ethnic minorities. Observation was concentrated at busy times of the day and night and panda car patrols, foot patrols and Home Beat officers were all represented in the sample.

Two different observers worked in each of the three forces; all were aged between 25 and 30, two female and four male. They observed a total of 149 constables during 238 sessions of observation (a session usually lasting 4-5 hours). Officers were accompanied only during the time they spent away from the police station.

The observers adopted as unobtrusive a role as possible, and there was little impression that officers were inhibited by their presence once some initial reticence wore off. A minimum of information was recorded while in the field, in the form of brief notes. At the end of each session these notes were expanded on to a two page form for the session as a whole, plus a nine page 'contact form' for each encounter witnessed. In addition, a prose description of each encounter was written at this point.

Fleeting and extended encounters

It was recognised from the start of the project that many contacts would be very brief and largely non-problematic, for example, when officers were asked for time or directions. (In the British Crime Survey, Southgate and Ekblom (1984) found that one quarter of the public had made this type of approach to a police officer at least once in the previous year.) The potential of such contacts for affecting the quality of police-public relations may, though, be quite large when considered on a cumulative basis. Observers noted the general manner in which such contacts were handled, and recorded any particular problems which arose but these were few. Where this or any other contact involved more than three verbal exchanges between the parties, it was regarded as an 'extended' contact rather than a 'fleeting' one, and fuller details were recorded. Of the total number of 981 contacts on which information was recorded, three quarters were thus classified as 'extended'.

Types of encounter observed

The encounters which were observed during the study can be classified according to the central activity involved for the officer in each case. Classification even in these terms is not always straightforward, and simple descriptive labels can be deceptive. To give an extreme example, one encounter began as a burglary report but, on further investigation, it also involved a report of a suspected illegal immigrant and a domestic dispute. In such cases a code was allocated according to what seemed to be the predominant issue.

Table 2:1 The fifteen most common types of encounter

	%
Burglary investigations/reports	9
Vehicle stops	8
Police initiated social/casual conversations	8
Enquiries at domestic premises	7
Giving time or directions	5
Foot stops	4
Missing person reports	3
Public initiated social/casual conversations	3
Domestic disputes	3
Damage to private property/vehicles	3
Enquiries at business premises	2
Moving vehicles along	2
Complaints of rowdy youths/children	2
Enquiries from public about matters already in police hands	2
Assaults/fights	2
	(N = 981)

To capture the full flavour of patrol work, some one hundred categories were used. Table 2:1 lists the fifteen categories which arose most often, accounting for about two thirds of all the encounters observed. There is clearly no one type of encounter which can be said to predominate; the list emphasises once again just how varied police patrol work is, with the implied need for the constable to be very much a generalist in his approach to the job.

Table 2:2 gives a summary of frequencies for all the observed encounters, using broader categories than Table 2:1 and grouping them into public initiated and police initiated encounters.

Table 2:2 Summary of police and public initiated encounters

Police-initiated

	%
Stops of vehicles or pedestrians	12
Other enquiries	9
Social/casual contacts	8
Delivering messages	5
Moving along people or vehicles	3
Arrests	1
Total	38

Public-initiated

Burglaries/alarms/suspicious persons	13
Disturbances/disputes	11
Information offered/advice sought	10
Non-crime emergencies/calls for help	10
Thefts	6
Vandalism	4
Assaults/fights/obscene calls	3
Social/casual contacts	3
Total	60

(N.I. = 2%)   (N=981)

The main purpose in presenting these figures is as background to later chapters, but it is worth noting also that they confirm previous findings (eg Southgate and Ekblom, 1984) in regard to the overall balance between public-initiated and police-initiated contacts, with 60% being initiated by the public. Patrol work as observed in the study clearly involved significant elements of responding to crime reports, of dealing with public order issues and of coping with other incidents arising. The figures are based only on the time which patrol officers spent outside of the police station.

Analysis of problems

The focus of the study upon the problematic aspects of police patrol work does not simply involve a distinction between problematic and non-problematic types

9

of encounter. By their nature, some of those listed in Tables 2:1 and 2:2 are indeed more likely than others to be complex and ambiguous. But what the study also showed is that problematic issues do not, in fact, arise just in certain types of encounters — domestic disputes, perhaps — but in all kinds of encounters, including those which many police officers assume can be dealt with strictly 'by the book'.

It is important to say something at this point about how 'problem' areas were identified. The methods used for this purpose were developed from the observer debriefing sessions conducted during the pre-testing and piloting work. At these sessions it became obvious that a central role in the analysis and interpretation of the data could actually be played at such meetings. Thus, at weekly or fortnightly intervals throughout the fieldwork period, observers met the researchers to discuss at length what they had observed. Each meeting was also attended by one of a series of middle ranking police officers, often with some training involvement. This brought a valuable dimension to the discussions, reminding the researchers of some of the practical and organisational constraints upon the behaviour of constables, and pointing the way to training implications. The main function of these meetings was to develop a cumulative list of 'hypotheses' or problems relating to the human relations side of encounters. The final list included several hundred of these, which were eventually refined into the problem areas discussed in the following chapters. The evidence for statements made in these chapters is based upon statistical analyses, discussions at the meetings, and the written records of encounters provided by observers; but the second of these was by far the most fruitful.

In looking at how police and public interacted and, in particular, in judging the appropriateness of police words and actions, it was often necessary to make some kind of evaluative judgement. This raises a dilemma which could be pursued at some length though the intention here is to treat it simply as a methodological point. Although it is possible, in simple terms, to conceive of the police officer as acting in a totally impartial and objective manner, the reality is that in almost every case he uses some degree of discretion or personal judgement. How, then, to judge what he does? Are his actions to be judged by the standards of his colleagues in the rank and file? his supervisors? the top managers of his force? or the general public (or some section of that public)? Or is there some other standard to apply? The law itself can provide no general answer to this question but it comes fairly close by providing the concept of the 'reasonable' man or woman. In judging the behaviour they saw, then, the research team sought to look at it through the eyes of such a 'reasonable' person.

For the sake of brevity, all police officers are referred to as 'he' in the text. This seems appropriate to the extent that the great majority of police officers are male: one in eight of the officers in the sample were female, reflecting fairly closely the overall proportions in the forces concerned.

3 Expectations

This chapter provides some of the necessary context for those which follow by looking briefly at the sort of expectations which police officers and the public bring to their encounters. People in all occupations have expectations about what their job will be like, based upon previous experience, the experience of others, training, the rules of the job, and so on. These expectations help reduce the uncertainty of life and make routine decision making easier.

In observing police officers it soon becomes clear that what they do when they meet the public is in large part a reflection of their expectations, both in general about the way their job should be done and specifically in relation to particular circumstances. Officers have their own expectations about encounters, there are also general legal and social norms to be followed, and there are the expectations of individual members of the public to take account of. All these bear upon the way the public and the police behave towards each other in encounters.

General expectations

After working in a particular area for a while an officer inevitably develops his own ideas about the people who live there and its other characteristics. An understanding of the neighbourhood and the people in it is clearly highly desirable if he is to do the best job. But there are two ways in which this understanding can develop. Ideally it should lead into a sensitivity to the people and problems of the area and some ability to cope with those problems, either by direct police action, by helping people to help themselves or by referring problems to alternative agencies. On the other hand, there can be difficulties for everyone, including the police, if local knowledge and understanding goes no further than having stereotyped views about the people in the area and the way they behave. One of the classic examples of stereotyping is the assumption that West Indian youths running or carrying a bag are up to no good (Cases 18, 21). It must be said that a number of officers seemed to avoid contact with black suspects — and, by extension, with other black people — because they were aware how sensitive this could be. They felt genuinely confused as to just what was expected of them; should they turn a blind eye for fear of provoking a riot if they stopped a black suspect? Or should they risk being called racists for pursuing them?

There were other cases of stereotyping, though not racial; these were often much less obvious — but equally mistaken and potentially harmful to the quality of policing. This problem of stereotyping by police officers has been noted for some

11

time. Reiner (1985) describes it in terms of the 'typical' officer's views of some of his client groups, identifying seven categories. These are, he says, "generated by their power to cause problems, and their congruency to the police value system." They are: *(i)* Good class villains (professional criminals); *(ii)* Police property (low status, powerless groups which the majority in society do not wish to be associated with, including vagrants, the unemployed, ethnic minorities, political activists etc); *(iii)* Rubbish (people from group *(ii)* making calls for police help, typically domestic disputes); *(iv)* Challengers (doctors, lawyers, social workers with power and information allowing them to challenge police control of their 'property'); *(v)* Disarmers (women, children, the elderly or others who may get special sympathy if they complain about how police treat them, thereby weakening the police); *(vi)* Do-gooders (anti-police activists such as NCCL); *(vii)* Politicians (ivory tower idealists).

In the absence of hard information about the people they are going to meet officers may fall back on these or other stereotypes, and they may still refer to such stereotypes even once they have seen the people involved. Police officers must have some knowledge of society and the groups within it, but there are two main pitfalls here. First, if they look at everyone they encounter with a view to labelling them and treating them in a predefined manner they will sometimes mislabel with possibly serious consequences. Second, the sorts of category listed above help perpetuate an 'us and them' mentality by defining people in terms of how much trouble they are likely to cause the officer.

Police officers know some members of the public better than others, and vice versa, and the progress of a particular encounter can reflect these previous relationships. Officers may know people as individuals, as members of a group or class of person, as residents in a particular area, as villains, or as law-abiding citizens. In the study as a whole, the officer seemed to have some prior acquaintance with members of the public in at least one in seven encounters. Where the relationship is not on a personal basis there are, of course, dangers of stereotyping, and if a person is previously known to the officer as an offender or other source of trouble to the police, then the officers may be less polite to that person or treat him in a way not justified by the circumstances. Likewise, greater credence tends to be given to a complainant in the first instance than to a person identified as a suspect or offender. It was certainly clear that, in general, certain classes of person were regarded by officers as 'deserving' or 'non-deserving' according to the previous experiences of the officer — or his colleagues — with that person or with someone seen as similar.

In their relations with 'non-villains', officers show certain preferences, tending to cultivate those in more visible positions, such as shopkeepers, or those in some semi-official capacity such as security guard or doorkeeper. Sometimes they cultivate people who can do them small professional or personal favours or give them useful information about local troublemakers.

Having had previous conversations with a person, the constable can assume a shared knowledge of some pieces of information or police procedure. He must be careful about this though, because it may be a wrong assumption and lead to confusion.

People who are in frequent social or casual contact with police officers may also have their own assumptions and expectations. One of these is that they may treat other officers with the same familiarity as the ones they know well. This may or may not be acceptable to the constable involved; if it is not, there may be confusion and bad feeling.

Law enforcement

There is a tension in policing between a desire to see the job as one of dealing with crime, and the reality that much of the demand for police service involves issues of public order, of civil law or miscellaneous matters best described as 'social service' problems. Observers noted a tendency for some officers to have informal specialisms, sometimes to the extent that other officers might turn to them for advice on that subject. Such interests normally appeared to involve aspects of the law rather than any kind of social problem, though there were some officers who showed an interest in offering advice to the public on non-crime issues. Where officers had special interests this was reflected in a more rapid response to any call which offered the chance of dealing with these interests. By the same token there was also a tendency to ignore or avoid jobs which offered minimal interest. This is not to say that social service problems were consistently ignored; indeed, a considerable amount of time was spent dealing with such matters. But many did so less readily. Thus, for example, police officers find domestics 'messy' to deal with and likely to be inconclusive for all involved, whereas going to a burglary is much closer to the 'crime fighting' concept of policing. (None of the observers working on the study were specialists in police research or even acquainted with the literature, but it was quite striking to note how quickly they began to comment on this preference among the officers they observed.)

The chance of enforcing the criminal law is one stimulus to which the officer responds. Another factor is simply whether there is any law which the officer thinks it likely he will be able to use. This can include traffic or public order law as well as criminal law. There are certain types of law which are actually very difficult for the average officer to enforce with confidence unless his knowledge is exceptional. Some do take an interest in enforcing such laws because by learning about it they can carve a niche for themselves and others will defer to their specialist knowledge. Traffic law is a prime example of this, to the extent that some officers try to avoid it as much as possible, heavy goods vehicle regulations being notorious in this respect.

It was sometimes unclear whether, when stopping a vehicle, it was a criminal or a traffic law violation the officer suspected. In practice, suspicion of one may be used as a way into the investigation of the other. So much public contact with the police now takes place within the context of traffic law enforcement, and the unfavourable views of the police which may result can well be counterproductive to efforts to secure cooperation in enforcing criminal law.

Racism

Evidence of overtly racist police behaviour was rarely observed in the study. In common with the PSI study (Smith and Gray, 1983) there were some occasions when officers used racist language amongst themselves or to the observers, or expressed views highly critical of ethnic minorities (Cases 4, 6, 20). But these were not normally reflected in actual words or behaviour towards minorities. (Case study 3, however, provides one possible exception to this.) The sceptic will be unsurprised by this finding, and argue that such behaviour would be deliberately avoided in front of observers. On the face of it, this does seem possible, but there are several reasons to modify this view. First, other observational studies have seen very clear evidence of discriminatory behaviour; Reiss (1971), for example, found this. Second, in the present study and others, police under observation have behaved in ways which were not racist, but were unprofessional in other respects, suggesting that the observer's presence did not always lead to 'best' behaviour. Third, the use of racist language in the presence of observers suggests a general lack of concern about the observer's opinion.

There may, however, be one factor beyond all these which minimises the apparent amount of police racism. Although some 15% of the encounters involved one or more ethnic minority members of the public it was suggested to observers by some officers that there was generally less contact than there might be. Police officers, they said, were nowadays so confused about how they were supposed to treat ethnic minorities (on the one hand they saw black youths and left wing politicians being hostile towards them while on the other hand was the liberal establishment telling them to behave more tolerantly to such people) that they avoided contact with them as much as possible so as to avoid the dilemma, especially where there might be hostility which could lead to complaints about their behaviour.

Public expectations

The nature of an encounter can be pre-conditioned by public expectations as well as by those of the police. The public do have very definite expectations as to what the police should do and how they should behave, and some thought was given to ways in which public views of encounters could be studied. But this was not pursued because of the various methodological and resource problems involved.

The public were not generally observed before or after the encounter itself or questioned at any stage, so that not a great deal can be concluded about their attitudes. But the fact that a person reports a problem to the police shows that they do have expectations that this is something the police should know about and may act upon. The frequency with which officers 'resolved' encounters by saying they could do nothing about the problem was encouragingly low: in only 1% of encounters did the officer bluntly say there was nothing the police could do, while in a further 3% he pointed out that police action was not needed or that people could handle the matter themselves. This says nothing about whether there would have been a better way of dealing with the issue, or whether other actions the police took were good ones, but it does suggest that the great majority of people using police services are correct in expecting that the police can and will do something rather than turn them away.

Summary

The nature of an encounter between police and public can be conditioned by any number of factors, not least the pattern of expectations which the two parties hold about the other. Policemen and members of the public each believe that the other ought to behave in certain ways towards them when they meet or when certain circumstances arise. Frequently, these expectations are disappointed, though experience often prepares them for this. The observers were well placed to take account of police expectations, and these became very clear during the course of fieldwork. Officers clearly felt that certain members of the population were either more or less deserving of their help than others, or posed more or less of a problem to them. They were generally more keen to deal with matters of law than of order maintenance or social service. In some cases it was clear than these preconceptions and expectations did affect the quality of service the public received. But it would be a mistake to assume that this will always be the case.

4 Entering the encounter

It was suggested earlier that encounters should be seen as processes rather than events, and reference was made in particular to the model proposed by Bayley and Bittner (1985) setting out the technical choices open to officers at each of three stages: contact, processing and exit. The rest of this report uses the same broad three part framework but looks primarily at the human relations issues likely to arise at each stage.

In most cases the actions taken by officers did seem to be related to the three broad stages. But the problems which officers faced and the choices they could make about them occurred in varying sequences, so that the officer might find himself faced with a typical 'exit' problem at the 'contact' stage, and a 'processing' problem might be present the whole way through. The three stage classification of problems is thus perhaps more of a conceptual device than a description of reality. But it provides a framework for examining the often rather diverse collection of issues raised in the course of the observations, and it can also provide a structure for leading police recruits to an understanding of the problems they will face during encounters.

At each of the three stages of the encounter measures were recorded of several indicators of police and public behaviour. These were drawn from previous studies (especially McIver and Parks, 1983) and included the demeanour and tone of voice of both parties, the apparent emotional state of the citizen, and any indications of satisfaction or dissatisfaction with the officer. Analysis of the scores on these indicators showed several things. First, three quarters of all encounters were conducted in a calm, polite and friendly manner; rudeness and hostility were uncommon and voices were rarely raised. Second, although not strongly pronounced, there was some tendency for friendly behaviour to increase on both sides during the course of the encounter. Third, officers tended to confine themselves to being businesslike and friendly, whereas the public displayed a wider range of behaviour.

The foregoing gives an overall impression of what relationships were like during the encounters observed. In order to examine them in more detail, this chapter and the two following look, in turn, at the three stages of entry, processing and exit. The rest of the current chapter considers some of the problems which can arise at the stage where the officer first approaches an encounter and then comes into contact with the citizen. These include lack of information, giving advance warnings, the manner of arriving, and agreeing the purpose of the encounter.

17

Lack of information

Some 73% of the encounters witnessed were initiated while the officer was patrolling, 11% while he was dealing with some other matter, and 15% while he was at the police station. Just over half began in response to a message from the radio controller, just over a third were initiated by the officer himself, and one in eight were directly instigated by a member of the public.

In only one in fifty encounters was any warning given to the officer as to the likely ease, danger or difficulty of the encounter. In one in seven some comment was made to a colleague or to the observer before arriving about the people or the place the officer was about to visit. (Though often, of course, there was no time for him to do so.) By the end of the encounter though, it became clear to the observer in 15% of encounters that the officer had some prior acquaintance with those involved, as previous offenders or suspects (3%) complainants (4%), in their professional capacity (2%) or in some other way.

It seems clear, then, that in most cases when an officer begins an encounter he has very limited information on which to base his expectations and to start formulating tentative ideas as to how it might be handled. Whether he is responding to a radio message, initiating a contact himself on the spot or responding to a direct approach from a member of the public he may be equally short of vital information. In the last two cases he has to start thinking even more quickly about what is involved and what he has to do.

While the officer may not, and should not wish to, prejudge at this stage just how the problem should be resolved, it is important not to start off on the wrong foot through being ill informed. In the absence of good information the danger is that he will fall back on stereotypes and begin the encounter with preconceptions which turn out to be totally misguided.

Assuming that no information (apart, sometimes, from an address) or only very limited information is available, how should the officer approach a call? Various ways were observed in which officers coped with this lack of knowledge. Some would be honest about their ignorance and simply ask the person to tell them what the problem was. Some would ask an open question: "Hello, what's the problem?" (Cases 24, 26) — without revealing a complete lack of knowledge as to what the problem was. Some would try to bluff their way, hoping that the person would reveal more without them asking.

Shortage of information at this point is a problem noted by previous research (Ekblom and Heal, 1982). There is often, of course, no time for the officer to acquire better information before arriving at the scene. In four out of ten encounters there was no time to do so because he was on the spot rather than being despatched to the scene, and in nearly all the rest there was less than ten minutes between being informed of the call and arrival at the scene. In fewer than one in ten encounters was there longer than this for the officer to prepare himself.

While part of this time problem arises from the public demand on police services, it may also result from assumptions about the desirability of fast response as a general guiding principle. A 'graded response' system of dealing with calls could help here: in judging the urgency of response appropriate to a particular call the controller might then take into account the time needed for obtaining extra information or passing such information on to the attending officer rather than simply aiming to deal with everything in the quickest possible time.

The amount of preparation needed may not be very great in most cases, but, where there is time in hand, there may be scope for establishing further facts. This can be partly a task for the officer, though in most cases he is dependent on radio contact with the controller for clarification. Even when he does ask for such further information it may not be forthcoming, so that the solution may lie very largely out of his hands. What is important is that the patrolling constable is made aware of the need to seek adequate information, either via the controller or by checking directly with the collator or other colleagues who may have information.

Advance warnings

In some cases the information available to the controller and/or patrol officer was quite ample or provided cues, at least, as to how matters might be handled. But these cues were not always taken. The best examples of this were cases where officers were sent to visit people known to be elderly or infirm. The shock of an officer appearing unannounced on the doorstep, possibly late at night, can be quite serious for some such people, and the idea of telephoning them to forewarn of the visit is one which needs serious consideration. At present, it rarely seems to be considered as an option.

Related to this (and considered later) is the question of the embarrassment for some people in being seen to have the police call or to be seen being questioned. The police cannot, and for most purposes, should not try to become invisible, but they should be more aware of the problem which their arrival may create for some members of the public.

Arrival

The manner of arrival at and initiation of an encounter is something with probably greater significance for the public than for the police. For most people the arrival of a policeman is a unique, possibly dramatic and frightening event but, for the officer himself, it is routine and non problematic. In its most extreme form the problem of the arrival is typified by the 'lights and siren' syndrome, with the patrol car arriving at speed, screeching to a halt, officers jumping out and rushing into action. A rapid response (with the use of lights and sirens if the officer was in a car) was involved in 7% of the encounters studied, a prompt (but not rapid) response occurred in 38%, and a slow or delayed response in 16% of instances. In the remaining encounters – nearly four out of ten of the total – the officer was already on the spot because he himself had initiated contact or had been approached by someone in the street.

Some would question whether rapid response is ever appropriate; there are certainly doubts about its contribution to effective law enforcement (Pate *et al*., 1976). But it performs an important function for the police officer. Holdaway (1977), for example, has described how it is used by officers as a means of generating excitement. It may cut the odd moment from the journey time and its justification is that this could be crucial; very occasionally this might be so, but this has to be set against the serious danger to pedestrians and other traffic and the low probability of catching a wrongdoer. There certainly seems little logic in arriving at a call in such a manner; it can warn off offenders still present, attract unwanted crowds, and raise the tension and anxiety for innocent people involved.

Even without such obvious signs, it is possible to arrive at a call by car in an aggressive and offensive manner. This may result partly from the type of car involved. Some officers made clear their disgust at having to drive small cars such as are used for most beat patrol rather than the more stylish vehicles of the traffic patrols, and they seemed to compensate for this by driving conspicuously and aggressively and by parking sometimes in very conspicuous and obstructive ways. Young men and motor vehicles can form a dangerous combination; the fact that the young men are in police uniforms does not entirely remove that problem.

Entry

The first stage of the encounter most commonly (43%) took place in the street or other public open place, but a wide range of other locations was involved: private homes or gardens 31%, commercial premises or spaces 13%, shared internal or external residential spaces 6%, public buildings 4% and police cars or police stations 3%. Very rarely (3% of encounters) was there major difficulty in locating a call, or in gaining access to a building to deal with it (just over 1%).

The main individual or group involved were male in 60% of encounters, female in 33% and groups of mixed sex in 6%. Only 7% were under 15, 26% were under 25, and 66% were under 45. 85% were white, 8% West Indian, 5% Asian and 3% of either other ethnic groups or a mixed group. A number of other characteristics were noted which might possibly have been used as visual cues by officers in summing up an individual, particularly on first sight. People were dishevelled or dirty in 18% of encounters, and 4% were showing evidence of drink or drugs. The behaviour or speech of 3% suggested some evidence of mental disorder, while 3% had some physical handicap and 1% were deaf. All but 2% spoke clear English.

The member of the public involved at the first stage took a number of different roles: 36% were victims or complainants of a crime or some other plight, 21%

were suspects or offenders, 21% were friends, helpers, witnesses or others with useful information, 9% were social/casual aquaintances of the officer, 7% were people seeking help or advice on minor matters, 5% were officials of a firm or organisation.

One quarter of encounters involved more than one member of the public at the first stage, though only 4% involved more than three people. In 15% of cases there were bystanders present, but only 4% of the time did this involve more than three people, and in 2% there were 10 or more people watching.

In one quarter of the encounters there were two or more constables present at the scene at this stage, and there were supervisory officers present in 2% of cases. (At some stage in the proceedings, supervisors were present at 3% of encounters, but they nearly always simply observed, or participated without actually taking over control from the constable.) In a very few cases there were others involved, such as ambulancemen, firemen, social workers or other 'official' helpers.

Agreeing the purpose of the encounter

An important thing to be established as early as possible in the encounter is a common understanding between officer and citizen as to what the encounter is about. This can be achieved in different ways, which may vary in difficulty depending on the nature of the issue and other factors, but there will normally be a point in the initial phase of the encounter where its 'terms' are defined. Where this does not happen the encounter is likely to be particularly difficult to deal with.

The officers observed often failed to explain their purpose clearly. Just how they should introduce themselves and come to the point will vary with the issue involved, and what is important is that the officer be sensitive to this, rather than simply treating everything in the same way just because it is 'all routine' to him. Delivering a fairly mundane message is a different task from delivering news of a death or other serious event; making a house to house enquiry is different from stopping someone in the street. Very different styles of behaviour may be needed for each of these or other tasks. A constable knocking at a door making house to house enquiries may himself know why he is doing it, but must not forget that the person who answers the door most likely does not, and must be treated politely and patiently. Similarly, a person being stopped in a car or on foot must be told why if he is to be expected to cooperate at all willingly.

Officers can very easily be tempted to play upon the citizen's uncertainty; this gives them at least a short term advantage and it gives them time. A slow pace in initiating and processing a vehicle stop, for example, can raise tension in the driver, making him more vulnerable to control by the officer. In such instances it may suit the officer's purpose not to come straight to the point. A simple device with a suspected drunken driver is to start by asking him what his car number is in order to covertly smell his breath, rather than risk putting him on the defensive

21

immediately by announcing his suspicions. It would be unrealistic to demand that the police never resort to 'trick questions' or circuitous conversations in their investigations of offences. But the principle to establish is that this should be done only if unavoidable, and should certainly not be done where the person involved is clearly innocent of any offence.

Tedious though it may be, some explanation may also be called for to anyone at whose door a constable knocks in error. This can often happen when responding to a call without proper information; names, street names or numbers are often wrongly given, transmitted or received by the time they reach the constable. Poor numbering can also be confusing, so that preliminary enquiries may get made almost at random to help clarify directions. A full explanation at every such address may not be practicable, but as far as those living there are concerned they have been approached by the police and are entitled to a reasonable explanation, politely given. Too often this is neglected. It illustrates a more general danger of officers assuming that what is routine or common understanding to themselves has only the same mundane significance to members of the public. There is scope for much harm to public relations if this simple fact is neglected.

In responding to a call the first thing an officer must do is to establish that he is at the right address and has located the right person. Once this is achieved, the onus is upon the citizen to explain the problem, but the officer must try to elicit the sort of explanation which will provide the most useful information. The person may be a crime victim, a participant in a domestic dispute, or someone suffering from some other problem; vandalism or rowdy youths, for example. But, whatever it is, the first thing the officer must do is listen. If he prejudges the situation wrongly and then takes a stand in favour of one party or another he could be getting into considerable trouble himself, losing credibility and authority with the other party or ultimately with all those people involved on whatever side.

When it is the officer who initiates an encounter the onus is upon him to explain his presence. In most such cases he will be either stopping someone on foot or in a vehicle, calling at their premises to make some enquiry, or calling to deliver some kind of message. In some ways the last is the most difficult to handle, for it can involve the delivery of bad news. When breaking bad news there are essentially two approaches used by constables; coming straight out with it, or 'fudging' the issue by pretending they only know part of the story, or that they do not know the latest developments. Just which approach should be used depends partly on a judgement of the audience and how they will take it. Depending on the information to be given and the person it is to be given to there may sometimes be a case for telephoning, either as a substitute for a personal visit or as an advance warning that a constable will be calling.

In the case of stops of pedestrians or drivers, the manner of starting an encounter will be rather different. The officer must be sufficiently authoritative to show that he is to be taken seriously right from the beginning but, at the same time, he must be very careful not to generate resentment. This can happen very easily, particularly when the citizen knows – or believes – that he is innocent. There is clearly scope for a great deal of misunderstanding at this point; mostly from the citizen, but also from the officer. What is crucial at this point is that the citizen is not seen to be challenging the authority of the officer to stop and question him. Although there may be resentment in a vehicle stop, there is rather less ambiguity present: it is clear to the driver in most cases that he has been stopped because of some suspicion of a driving or vehicle offence. Even if that is not the primary purpose for the stop the officer may act at first as though it is, so that there is immediately some structure to the encounter to which both sides can relate.

Foot stops are different; their purpose is not immediately evident, but the assumption will tend to be that a criminal offence is suspected which is, generally, more serious than a vehicle offence, so that there is potentially more at stake for the citizen. The physical spaces involved are less clearly defined than when a driver is stopped. Once the officer approaches he has the driver more or less physically under his control so long as he remains in the car. But a pedestrian may not choose to stop or to stand still just where the officer would prefer him to; if he moves around a lot this gives the officer less immediate control of the situation unless he decides to exert authority quite openly by ordering the person to keep still.

Broadly speaking, what is being agreed at the start of an encounter is whether the citizen is doing something at the request/demand of the officer or whether the officer is doing something for the citizen. Things can become difficult for the officer to manage smoothly if this role relationship then has to change, particularly if it means an initially 'innocent' person becoming a suspect for an offence. For example, some people who report that their electricity or gas meters have been broken into actually turn out to have done it themselves, and this kind of role reversal may then take place.

Opening manner

It is easy for an officer's opening manner to betray his expectations of the other's reaction to him. If he expects hostility and behaves at first as if it has already been shown, then it probably will be. It was obvious that officers retained better control of the situation and friendlier relations prevailed where the officer began on a friendly note rather than an unfriendly one. If he began in a more hostile way it was then more difficult for him to 'climb down' than it was for him to 'turn on the heat' if it subsequently seemed justified even though he had begun in a friendly manner.

The attitude an officer should take to a suspect is, of course, a difficult issue. The experience of being arrested is certainly traumatic for all but the most hardened villain, whether that person is guilty or not, and some resistance or hostility will not be uncommon. Arrests were observed fairly rarely in the study (Cases 9, 12, 25); an arrest was the central activity occasioning only 11 encounters and was involved at some stage of the encounter in a total of 36 altogether (less than 4% of the total). There were many more occasions when people were being questioned with the expressed or implied suspicion that they might be guilty of some offence. Thus, 81 vehicle stops and 39 foot stops were observed, vehicle stops being the second largest category of encounters after burglary investigations.

Control of encounters is an important issue for the officer from the start of an encounter onwards, but the danger is that he overreacts to the demands of maintaining order and obtaining respect, seeing these as ends in themselves, whereas they are mostly just prerequisites for the more important tasks of seeking information and resolving the problem. There is a difficult balance here, but one which needs more thought by trainers and patrol officers. This issue is considered in some detail in the following chapter.

Summary

This chapter has looked at some of the problems in the entry stage of an encounter. It described how encounters arose, who was involved and where they took place. In the great majority of cases the officer had no prior acquaintance with the person involved and very little information about the circumstances. It is suggested that if less emphasis could be put upon maximising the speed of response to some calls, officers might arrive better equipped to deal with them; in a few cases this very speed may have harmful effects upon police-public relations. Very important at the entry stage is to establish a mutual understanding as to why officer and citizen have come together. This is sometimes obvious, but there are dangers in assuming this to be so to both parties. Depending on how and why the encounter is initiated, the officer must take steps to achieve a clear understanding on both sides. If this is not done there may be later confusion and needless annoyance may be caused. He should also bear in mind that what may seem mundane to himself can be anything but mundane for some members of the public.

5 Processing the encounter

This chapter discusses issues which arise during processing an encounter. Broadly, this encompasses everything which takes place after the initial contact has been established and before the officer resolves (or fails to resolve) whatever problem has been at issue and leaves the scene. Two main topics are included here: respect for people's feelings, and deference and control. One further issue considered is that of how paperwork and administrative duties can impinge upon encounters.

(1) Respecting people's feelings

Encounters with the police are likely to involve a range of emotions for members of the public. Sometimes these are positive ones such as relief or reassurance, but often they are more negative: anxiety, guilt, worry, hostility, distrust, resentment and nervousness are all among the terms which might apply from time to time. Embarrassment is one term which probably covers many of these and other emotions. This term is used with a fairly broad meaning in the following paragraphs rather than trying to be overly precise in identifying particular shades of emotions for, without extended questioning of individuals, it would have been impossible to arrive at a high degree of precision in describing the emotions witnessed.

One thing which previous studies have shown (Ekblom and Heal, 1982; Jones, 1985) is that although it may be important for officers to do what they can towards solving a crime and pursuing an offender, what victims put equal store by is the amount of sympathy and emotional help which is offered to them. They want officers to realise not just the legal but the emotional hurt they have suffered, and to treat it for them. Observers in the present study certainly noted that, where officers were putting effort into this side of their dealings with crime victims, it was appreciated by those people and encounters seemed to go more smoothly. Generalising from the example of victimisation, it seems likely that public satisfaction with police service will be greater in most other situations if the officer is able to show the public that he understands the problems they face and is sensitive to their feelings.

Various examples were witnessed of behaviour which was insensitive to the public and could mostly be avoided. Offensive language was almost never heard used directly to people's faces, but abusive remarks were sometimes made about people in the presence of third parties (additional to the observer).

Two general points relating to sensitivity to people's feelings were very clear from the observations. First, officers must be seen to be listening to what people tell them. This seems fairly obvious, but there are many things officers do — particularly not looking at them or seeming to respond to what they say — which can make it appear they are not listening, even though they often are. A further point here is that by looking at a person while listening in the first stages of an encounter, the officer can also watch for visual clues to their thoughts and behaviour.

The second general point is that encounters starting with a friendly manner from the officer are much easier to handle, even if they have to become more serious later. If the officer starts off in an unfriendly and hostile manner it is more difficult for him to then become friendly later on if matters turn out to be less serious than he first thought.

The degree of sensitivity shown by an officer is likely to vary according to the character of the officer, the nature of the problem at hand, and the character of the citizen, including the role in which circumstances have cast that person. In general, it was clear that officers who were of a friendly and outgoing disposition found it easier to get on well with people; age and experience also helped in this respect.

Although officers may be well aware of the emotional traumas suffered by some of the people they are speaking to, this in itself does not equip them to respond helpfully to these traumas. One misguided response to victimisation which was seen was to tell victims gory tales of previous police cases, intended to demonstrate that 'there is always someone worse off than yourself'. Another was to make speculative comments about the likely progress of the case, or the future actions of the offender; these remarks may represent for the officer simply a mundane account of police matters. They show insensitivity because the officer is trying to get people to see things from his point of view rather than showing them that he understands theirs. But for the victim such comments can raise anxiety yet further. One piece of 'speculation' along these lines which might be useful is to stress how unlikely it is that the offender will strike them again. In many cases this will be true, though sometimes it may not and, in any case, this must always be balanced against the need to remain vigilant and take appropriate preventive action.

While the emotional suffering of burglary, sexual assault and other serious physical assault victims is not difficult to imagine, officers too often seem to overlook the problem of victims of apparently lesser offences. For many people, for example, even a minor assault leaving no clear marks can be extremely distressing. For the officer to make little response to this, or to say it is 'only' a common assault is not helpful if to that person it has caused extreme distress. Victims are sometimes very agitated. On one occasion a victim kept moving nervously and quickly around the house, seeming to be forever walking away from the officer and causing him some irritation. In fact all she was doing was continuing to check her property for further loss or damage. But the officer was torn between chasing around after her — rather a threat to his dignity — and standing still and shouting to make himself heard at a distance; neither solution very satisfactory from his point of view (Case 5).

Although at a more mundane and less emotionally fraught level, the manner in which casual enquiries in the street are dealt with can also raise problems. In Britain, if not in some other countries, there is a widespread expectation that police officers will be willing and helpful in response to requests for street directions, and this is the public's most common form of contact with the police (Southgate and Ekblom, 1984). The potential for either maintaining or damaging police public relations by the way such requests are handled is, therefore, immense and cannot afford to be overlooked. The response to such approaches should, obviously, be attentive and friendly; a loudly chattering police radio will be unhelpful here or, indeed, any other sign that the officer is not giving his full attention to the request being made. In responding, one mistake often noted was to give too much information too quickly. If the directions needed are rather complicated it may be difficult to make them simple but, once again, the officer must realise that what may be familiar or easy to him is not so for the citizen, so that he must be as patient and clear as possible.

Apart from the nature of the problem and the situation the citizen is in, the officer must try to determine what he can about the character of the person themselves. Some of this may be clear at first contact (though with some risk of stereotyping) but much will only be revealed during the course of the conversation. Premature judgement can be dangerous because it may lead the officer into statements or actions he may soon wish he had not made, by which time the damage may be done.

A favourite comment of police officers is that they try to talk to each member of the public in his/her own language. They do not mean by this that they literally speak in people's 'own language'; what they do is adjust their speech and behaviour according to whom they are dealing with. This may or may not work as intended and it will only do so if the person accepts the role into which the officer seems to have cast him. This involves the concept of deference, which is considered later in more detail.

Officers are sometimes confronted with people who are mentally disturbed, though the extent and nature of this is not always clear and great caution is needed. Some 3% of encounters in the study involved people showing obvious signs of mental disturbance and there could have been others where this was not obvious. Rules of thumb are particularly difficult to make here, but unless the person seems to be an immediate danger to themselves or others the officer is best advised to treat them with cautious trust, giving them the benefit of the doubt until he can get further evidence to clarify matters.

A particular problem which can arise for the officer is where he finds himself dealing professionally with a friend, relative or work acquaintance. In 3% of encounters this situation arose. It is mainly a problem when the person is in the suspect/offender role; this can cause considerable embarrassment for the officer if he has to apply some sanction. To avoid embarrassment to the parties and accusations of bias from others, the best solution to such a dilemma may be for the officer to hand over entirely to a colleague if one is available.

Both police and public may experience embarrassment in an encounter, though sometimes for different reasons. For the officer, a major source of embarrassment is people who are upset and distressed. About one encounter in every six involved a person who was clearly upset, so that this is something officers frequently have to cope with (Cases 5, 6, 24, 27). Often, though, the officer seemed to be ignoring the distress (Cases 5, 6). Conversations with police officers suggested that this did not mean they are unaware of the person's distress, but simply that they felt that the best way to cope with it was to try and ignore it. There are at least three reasons for doing this. (a) It may take much less time than if they discussed the person's feelings with them and made some effort to console them. (b) It may appear to the officer to be a way he can deal with someone who is simply 'being difficult'. (c) It may simply be a coping mechanism to protect the officer from too much emotional involvement and resultant stress. Whatever the reason, it looks to the citizen like insensitivity. Emotionally upset people are quite commonly encountered by police officers, so training should perhaps make more overt recognition of the need to prepare them for upsetting events and the emotions and behaviour they produce. Whatever referral facilities, such as victim support schemes, may be available to help victims of misfortune, the police officer is likely to remain in the front line, providing first aid to those with problems of many kinds. It should be recognised that the emotional demands are there and that it will be more satisfactory both for them and the public if police officers, like doctors, social workers or others who face human distress should be prepared by their training to cope with the problems.

Sexual offences and indecencies are very likely to cause embarrassment. There is a strong demand from various quarters for improved provision for victims of such offences, including more use of women officers and the provision of special facilities at police stations. The present study included a number of women officers, but only 1% of the encounters involved sexual and indecency offences (Cases 16, 17), so that there was not sufficient evidence to examine this issue in detail. Whatever specific arrangements may be made, though, officers of either sex are likely, from time to time, to find themselves having to cope with such victims, and they must be aware of and able to cope with the emotional as well as practical and legal aspects of the situations which face them.

A rather different source of embarrassment for the officer was the offering of gifts by the public, which he must refuse. This is difficult because, despite prohibitions on gratuities, some members of the public may actually be offended by a refusal. Grateful thanks but a politely explained refusal seem the most tactful response for the officer to make when faced with this. The one exception which can safely be made to this general rule is where cups of tea or other non-alcoholic beverages are concerned (see elsewhere).

Privacy

For the public their main source of embarrassment can simply be the fact of being seen with a police officer. Neither the guilty nor the innocent may wish to be seen being approached and questioned. For this to happen, or to have a policeman call at one's house is sufficiently unusual for most people that it can produce a curiosity on the part of neighbours; whatever the reason for the visit, there is always the feeling that the person is in some kind of trouble with the law or even that they are 'sneaking' to the police about their neighours. This can obviously cause intense embarrassment and the encounter may be far more productive for the officer if he takes steps to eliminate or reduce it. In one instance a publican was interviewed in his bar about a burglary he had suffered; this was done in full view and hearing of his customers, but it would have been quite easy for the officer to suggest they go into a private room. Conversations may be more productive if conducted out of public view and hearing unless, of course, the citizen prefers this not to happen. Where this is the case, though, care is needed that this does not result in the gathering of too many onlookers. The officer is in something of a cleft stick on this: if he interviews a person in public he may attract an unwanted audience, but if he takes the person to a private spot he may then be subject to later accusations of mistreatment.

Other examples were witnessed where quite personal details were being discussed within earshot of strangers when greater privacy was easily available. This principle must be considered whether the encounter is police or public initiated. In either case the officer needs information from the public and its flow may well be inhibited if there is an audience.

Police officers cannot and should not try to become invisible, but they should try to avoid causing embarrassment to innocent parties. A loud or aggressive approach will be particularly likely to draw attention to an encounter. Wherever the situation provides an opportunity for privacy which the public may appreciate, it will be best to take this. Greater use of the telephone might reduce the number of personal approaches which need to be made to deal with mundane matters.

Speaking through car windows

When officers are in a car and wish to speak to a pedestrian they do not always get out of the vehicle. It is common practice simply to draw up next to them and speak out of the car window (Case 28). Unfortunately, engine noise, traffic noise and distance mean that shouting, rather than speaking may be involved here, especially if the officer has to lean across his colleague to someone on the opposite side of the vehicle. Such shouting, although purely a practical necessity, can offend some people, and it can also look as if the officer cannot be bothered to get out of the car to speak to the person. The person outside the car may also be unable to make themselves heard without shouting. The end result of all this can be a difficult conversation for everyone with possible mishearing, misunderstanding, and bad feeling which could be avoided with a little trouble.

Body language

Body language can be crucial to police-public encounters, as with most human interactions. Because it is essentially visual, there was a limit to how much detail could usefully be recorded on paper in the study, but some note was made relating to gaze and proximity. In general, officers were rather more likely to look directly into the face of people they were speaking to than the reverse. As to proximity, in seven encounters out of ten the officer stood between 18 inches and four feet away from the citizen, while in 4% he stood closer and in 27% further away than this. Thus, nearly three quarters of encounters were conducted within what has been described as 'personal distance' rather than 'social distance' (Hall, 1966). It might be useful to conduct more detailed studies of such aspects of body language in police-public encounters, for there does seem to be some possibility that many of them could involve an 'invasion' of the citizen's 'personal space' by the officer. This may often be done quite unconsciously, and people may react to it unconsciously also. It is difficult to know from the present evidence how 'real' a problem this actually is for either party, but this is something which police officers and trainers could usefully explore.

Beyond these two general indicators, there is a great range of movements and gestures to which officers need to become sensitised. One example is the way officers indicate that they are being casual and relaxed — by taking off their helmet, unbuttoning their coat, putting their hands in their pockets or sitting down. There is no shortage of stories in police folklore telling of officers who calmed tense domestic disputes simply by displaying very relaxed body posture (Southgate, 1982; Bayley and Bittner, 1985). Such techniques can be very effective in the right circumstances, but if used at the wrong time may backfire, leaving the officer accused of slackness or indifference.

Officers need to recognise the effect which simply their personal appearance may have. For example, a large well built person inevitably looks more domineering than a short one and heavy winter uniforms also give this impression of bulk and forbiddingness. Large, heavy soled boots and 'hardware' dangling at the belt can convey similarly aggressive messages. Police officers know these things and sometimes use them deliberately, but in many cases it is inappropriate to convey this kind of message. There may be little an officer can do about his basic physique or even his uniform, but he should perhaps try to avoid moving his clothes or equipment in an aggressive way. One particular example of this were officers who — apparently as an 'absent minded' mannerism — stood punching one leather clad hand into the other, looking rather threatening as a result. (One police officer, unconnected with the study, commented that this is because police gloves tend to fit badly so that officers do this to try and stretch them!)

Signs which are transmitted largely unconsciously through body language can be difficult to pick up and respond to in the manner which is expected. This is true even of signs which are made quite consciously and deliberately. Problems were seen on some occasions when hand signals were made from within a police car to a person in another vehicle. Such messages are very easy to misread, even if the citizen wants to be cooperative, but the result may be that a police officer thinks he is being ignored or disobeyed. A problem with hand movements in everyday conversation is, again, that they may be misread by the other party because of cultural or individual differences.

Another aspect of body language is physical touch. In general, officers avoid this, but they did tend to touch certain types of people, primarily those who seemed to pose no real threat to them, such as children and old people. This mostly seemed to cause no problems, but led to problems on another occasion where a younger woman was touched, resulting in critical comments from onlookers (Case 14).

Personal radios

These are ever present and often very intrusive accoutrements to modern policing. The non police observer is amazed by the way officers appear to be able to listen to their radio with only half an ear yet still pick up any message which concerns them. Radios can be a problem for the public in some situations, though, and this is a fact to which some officers appear to be oblivious. When an officer attends a call he may or may not shut off or turn down his radio while talking to people. Those who do not may be seen as rude or insensitive by those people, because they may believe that he is not giving them his full attention. Indeed it is difficult to see how he can if he is still listening to the radio. Especially where the person is upset or nervous, to have the radio brusquely interrupting what they are trying to say is not at all helpful. Alternatively, the impression given may be that the person's problem is not important enough to pay full attention to, and the more diffident people may accept this and try to minimise their demands on the officer. In either case this is not as it should be; the radio should be one tool in good policing, not something which, intentionally or otherwise, dominates the officer's approach.

A further point about radios is that where a car radio is also being used, officers have two distractions instead of one. Cases were observed where officers avoided going back to the car until they had finished with one call in case they were summoned to another. One consequence of this was that they spent time in people's houses doing their paperwork.

Emotional people

In four out of five encounters dealt with, people were calm. But a significant minority were not: 13% of encounters involved someone who was upset, though not angry, and a further 3% who were angry as well. In only 5 instances was anyone actually physically aggressive. Dealing with angry people and with those

31

who are simply upset are rather different things. The upset but not angry person poses less of an immediate threat to order and safety, but is both a more common and, in some ways, more difficult problem. Some officers seemed to see no need to do anything about such emotions, but this apparent ignoring of the person's feelings seemed sometimes insensitive and shortsighted. The impression on some occasions was that the officer was showing no response to these public emotions not so much through insensitivity but because they embarrassed him. He was afraid to respond directly and openly to the person's emotions because that would seem like a display of weakness on his part. Police officers are by no means devoid of feelings: many will admit that, for example, one of the jobs they dread most is having to inform the family of a road accident fatality. But they react to the emotional challenges the job exposes them to by creating a 'hard shell' which protects them from becoming emotionally involved. But this so easily appears to the public as callousness.

The way to cope with upset people depends, of course, on why they are upset, which can have many causes. Most commonly it will be because they are victims of a crime, accident or other misfortune. In such cases an officer has to accomplish both 'practical' and 'emotional' tasks, though even the 'practical' tasks have emotional overtones. There may be movement or examination of injured people or damaged property to be achieved. This can be done in a spirit of 'it's all routine to me' or it can be done with tact and sensitivity. What has to be remembered is that what is routine to the officer is often unique, traumatic and frightening to the victim.

In many cases there will be limits to what can be done by the officer, and he then has to consider two things: first, whether anyone else can do more, whether legally (in matters of civil law), practically (such as repairing broken doors and windows) or emotionally (giving continuing counselling and support to victims). This can involve referrals to, for example, solicitors, local authorities or victim support schemes. He must then explain to the victim what he proposes to do, and the limits to the action which he or others can take. In doing so, he must take account of the second task, which is the provision of 'emotional first aid'. With or without the backup of a victim support scheme, it is still the police officer who must cope with victims' emotions in the first place and this is often poorly handled.

The emotions of an offender will be rather different, and possibly more immediately threatening to the officer, than will those of a victim. The temptation is to assume that because a person has broken the law their feelings deserve no consideration (Case 25). From a practical point of view this is shortsighted, because it may mean that the individual reacts by becoming more hostile and difficult for the officer to deal with. Also, not all suspects may turn out to be guilty upon further investigation, and the officer must be careful of acting as judge and jury in any case.

There are two broad classes of suspect: those who know they have broken the law and know when they have been found out, and those who do not realise they have committed an offence until the officer confronts them. In the first case there will, perhaps, need to be rather less concern about respect for feelings, though there is normally no need for officers to be heavy handed unless immediate resistance is offered (Case 15). In the second case, emotions may also include shock, guilt, embarrassment, resentment and open hostility to the facts the officer is confronting the person with (Case 9).

Another set of emotions may be found when dealing with the parties to a dispute. These can be particularly strong when a domestic dispute is involved (Cases 6, 24, 26). The primary objective which the probationary officer is trained to pursue in disputes is to restore the peace in the short term. This tends to be taken rather literally, so that there is not too much concern with anything beyond this. Although efforts have been made to develop counselling services to which those with problems can be referred, a research study in the United States (Sherman and Berk, 1984) has raised the possibility that the most effective way to reduce repeated wife battering may be simply to arrest the offending husband. Doubts about the generalisability of these findings have led to an expansion of research on this problem (National Institute of Justice, 1985). But, whatever may be concluded, it seems likely that the need for counselling services will continue and officers must be capable of recognising the need for referral, proposing it to disputants, and making arrangements for it to take place. Attempts to train police officers in handling domestic disputes themselves have not always met with great success (Bard, 1970), and it may be necessary to set fairly limited expectations as to how far a police constable can 'solve' such problems. But he is always likely to be the point of first contact and must be trained to handle that contact with sensitivity and understanding.

Sometimes, police officers seek to do little more than establish that no crime has occurred. Often it has not, but the complainant is not concerned, in the heat of the moment, with fine legal distinctions. It does not, therefore, help the public for the officer to say "this is not police business" and leave as soon as he can. Similarly, telling a distraught wife who has been abused on a Saturday night to "call your solicitor on Monday" is less than helpful. It is not always even said with any tact or proper explanation.

Repeat calls are common in domestic disputes, but because of shift changes it is often unlikely that the same officer will attend at the same address on consecutive occasions. This means that neither the police nor the citizens involved benefit from any continuity and developing understanding of the real nature of the underlying problems.

This continuity could be attempted by involving a Home Beat officer to monitor the case, or by referring it to a third party or agency who can maintain an extended contract.

Disputes may be encountered in a variety of other settings, often in a retail commercial context or between landlords and tenants. The latter can be especially complex because they can involve issues other than simply non-payment of rent where the landlord and tenant have a more personal relationship of some kind.

Finally, a common source of conflict to which police get called is where complaints arise about noise. Typical situations here are the West Indian 'blues' party which continues all night and sometimes for several days as well, the noisy group of children at play, and the playing of loud tapes and radios in streets and public areas.

(2) Control and deference

Although the particular tasks an officer must accomplish in an encounter will vary with the problem, there are certain things to be achieved in virtually every case. These have been defined by Sykes and Brent (1983) as seeking information, maintaining order, obtaining respect, and achieving an appropriate resolution. Others have looked at policing particularly in terms of its control function (eg Sichel, *et al*., 1978) though various views have been taken as to the centrality of the use of legitimate force in order to achieve this (Manning, 1977). There is general agreement, though, that the exercise of authority is central to the police mandate; without authority — and an acceptance of this authority by the public — the officer can achieve little. Most of the time this authority is not put to the test, but it is respect for it which maintains the peace and helps prevent crime. In all encounters then, one of the things the officer does is to exercise control, doing this by drawing on the corporate authority granted to the police service, and on his personal authority as an individual and as a member of that service.

At first sight it may appear that the officer rarely has to do very much by way of controlling people in encounters. This is true if control is seen simply in terms of restraining people from doing things the officer thinks they should not do. Under 4% of encounters were resolved by an arrest, and under 1% by threats of arrest or physical force. Officers raised their voices in only 5% of encounters.

But control may be exercised in three ways: physical restraint, the issuing of orders or threats, or the use of verbal reasoning and persuasion, the last of these being by far the most commonly observed. If persuasive talk is used effectively it may well be that the need for the other two forms of control is minimised, and that even better persuasive talk could reduce even further the small amount of conflict which does take place.

Although women officers may have less air of authority about them, it is sometimes claimed that they are better than men at conversation (Case 1). Those arguing for greater use of women officers in uniformed patrol work sometimes contrast the approach of the beefy male officer who stops a pub brawl by dragging out the aggressive drunk by the scruff of his neck, and that of the woman officer who simply goes in and talks him down with words alone. As most police work consists of having conversations women might, thus, be very well equipped for the job, though the counter argument is, of course, that police officers need physical strength and authority in reserve for unexpected emergencies, even though they may rarely make use of them. No clear impression emerged from the study to suggest that women were better than men in this respect. Although representative of the proportion of women officers in the police as a whole, the numbers in the sample were too few to enable systematic comparisons. Some officers — whichever their sex — find it easier than others to obtain respect and deference from the public, simply by virtue of their physical presence or their strength of personality. This can give an initial advantage and make people more inclined to listen to the officer, but what he says subsequently will probably count for more. Age and maturity will play a significant role here, but a good young officer must at least have the ability to know and develop his own strengths.

Officers have various expectations and assumptions about deference which affect the approach they have to encounters. In the study, pronounced deference was accorded to the officer in one of ten encounters, whereas the officers showed such deference on only one occasion in 100. Police officers assume that the public ought to respect their authority as upholders of the law, though the extent to which the public do so is not fully within officers' control; people may question their actions from the start, or the officer may behave in such a way as to provoke them into doing so at some point in the encounter (Case 25). Where police officers perceive a fundamental refusal to defer to their authority on the part of any particular group in society (black youths being the prime example), they may build up a basic resentment against the group and its members.

Within the police force, officers will defer to those of higher rank and longer experience, and among the public they will defer — other things being equal — to those of higher social status than themselves. Conversely, those lower down the social scale, and certainly those known to have had previous brushes with the law, are expected to show deference to police officers rather than to receive it. If anyone fails to behave in the expected manner this can be confusing for the officer and may lead him into the trap of reacting in a hostile manner. Some officers were particularly sensitive about respect for authority, and were predisposed to react against words or behaviour they saw as challenging that authority (Cases 12, 25).

A particular problem of deference arises in relations between young male police officers and young male members of the public. From the officer's point of view, the problem is, perhaps, one of distancing; the extent to which young men will defer to him may be inversely related to how similar to themselves he seems to be. An older man has years of developing his self-identity as a police officer behind him, but the young officer must somehow compensate for his lack of this. There are ways in which this is sometimes done, but they are not necessarily compatible with good policing and good public relations. But, however confident the young officer feels of his police identity, the young male citizen may still see him as another young male to be resisted if he offers any sort of challenge. Where there is

35

also a racial element — young black male citizens and young white male police — there are further factors working against the accordance of deference to the police officer.

It is genuinely difficult for young officers to compensate for lack of years and experience. They may have to work particularly hard at this by trying to avoid the kinds of behaviour which might appear immature or offensive, such as loud aggressive behaviour, assertive driving and building up tension between themselves and other young men.

Given the basic assumptions which officers appear to make about deference to their authority, there are various ways in which they are likely to act in order to establish, maintain, or reestablish this deference. One example of adjusting this balance can appear in vehicle stops. Because the car driver is to some extent 'protected' from control by the officer by being in his own 'personal space' this may reduce the need which he feels to defer to the authority of the officer standing outside the car. If the officer then asks the driver to get out of the vehicle he is both taking away this advantage, putting them both literally on an equal footing and giving himself some advantage by issuing an order with which the driver usually quickly complies. Although there may often be little clear rationale for this request it is normally complied with because it is the sort of request which people expect from an officer (Cases 13, 23). If the same approach is adopted in other situations, though, acceptance may be less. Giving a person orders to do something just for the sake of asserting authority over that person is undesirable and likely to be perceived as a gratuitous assertion of authority. The person may comply, but feel a loss of face and resulting resentment of the officer. If he does not comply, this creates instant conflict which can easily escalate even to the point ot physical violence. There is a temptation for some young and aggressive officers to 'set people up' in this way, pushing them by giving orders or making some other provocation, so that they can then directly challenge the officer's authority, which will then be promptly enforced (Smith and Gray, 1983).

Very many encounters involve the officer asking people questions. Again, this is usually accepted as the officer's job but, if it is resisted he is likely to react fairly strongly because he sees his duty being queried. Questioning is a very adaptable procedure. Questioning can be conducted in more or less forceful ways; questions can be made as easy or as difficult as the officer chooses, thus providing an excellent opportunity for him to maintain control. Also, the more information he gets from his questions, the more he knows about the citizen and what he has done, and this gives him power over that person. A reverse form of this occurs in encounters where it becomes clear that the citizen possesses information or understanding on the subject under discussion which is superior to that held by the officer. Both citizen and officer may need to tread carefully here if the officer is not to lose face or overreact in some way.

A slightly lesser dilemma for the officer is raised by those who, through ignorance or embarrassment rather than deliberate hostility, fail to take the police officer's presence seriously. Giggling young women, for example (Case 11), who do not seem to respond in any way the officer can understand to what he says to them, pose such a difficulty; there may seem to be no action he can take to secure the cooperation of such people. Indeed, if young people do choose to challenge the officer's authority and there is no serious breach of the law involved he often cannot fall back on law enforcing actions or threats of such. Even if an offence is involved it can still be difficult to act, because of the limits to the legal liability of young people.

Another type of deference problem is raised by the person who asks "Will this take long?" when stopped by an officer, typically for suspected driving or vehicle offences. This offers no direct challenge to the officer's right to act in the matter, but even if said in the most polite and deferential tones it does imply a challenge to the assumption that the officer has complete discretion over how the conversation is to be conducted. If the officer simply ignores the question or if he says that it will take as long as he finds necessary, then he has asserted his authority and may thereby get hostility, resentment or lack of cooperation. If he responds apologetically the danger is that the citizen thinks he has won — in the conversation if not in the final outcome — and this weakens the officer's position. Some form of compromise reply — "I have to do certain things but I'll do them as quickly as possible because I understand I am delaying you at an awkward time" — should keep the officer in control while giving the citizen a reasonably satisfactory answer at the same time.

Few people are too deferent; in only about one in ten encounters did deference to the officer go beyond being merely civil or friendly. Too much deference can, in fact, be seen by the officer as sarcasm, and the supposedly classic ploy of trying to ingratiate oneself with a constable by calling him "sergeant" is an extension of this principle which may well backfire on those who try to use it.

Controlling disputes

The handling of any sort of dispute provides a very obvious test of the officer's authority and his ability to control situations. Physical as well as verbal control may be involved, but little that is satisfactory is likely to be achieved if only the first is used. Not only does the officer have to quickly try to understand the substance and the dynamics of the dispute itself, but he has to take a role in it which takes account of these and takes over and controls the dispute. He then either resolves it or — too often — simply reduces it to an acceptable level of conflict or 'ceasefire' between the parties.

Very often a pair of officers will be sent to a dispute. This makes sense in terms of physical protection for the police themselves and for parties to the dispute, and it has value in that two disputants can be listened to separately. Assuming that a clear 'case' on each side can be identified from this, the officers can then come together in the presence of the disputants, put these cases as advocates and try to work towards some agreement.

37

Where the officer attends a dispute alone he must try to hear each side of it and then act in a 'chairman' role (Cases 24, 26, 27). In doing this great care is needed to avoid accusations of bias towards one side or the other. There are pitfalls here related to deference: there may be a temptation to defer to the views of the person who called the police in the first place, to the person of higher status (if this should apply), or to defer to the male in a male-female dispute (Case 26). These are fairly obvious pitfalls, but the study showed that they were easy for officers to fall into.

The best general approach of the officer to disputes — or to any tense situation — can be to adopt a very relaxed manner. This may not solve the problem; as the next chapter points out, there is some debate as to the best tactical choice to make in order to reduce the chance of a dispute recurring. But tension in the disputants is unlikely to be reduced if the officer himself appears tense.

Working with an audience

In handling many situations, one likely problem is that of audiences, especially where the encounter takes place out of doors. Crowds of spectators are one of the things which most concern police officers, particularly in black inner-city areas, the main fear being that they may attack an officer on his own or prevent him from questioning or arresting a suspect. The crowd which gathers around many police-public encounters may be initially impartial but soon start to take sides for or against the officer or other persons. This is common in the sequence of 'triggering' events leading up to outbreaks of public disorder (Field and Southgate, 1982). Officers are often now advised by their supervisors to avoid such arrests in areas highly exposed to public view.

In the study about one in 20 encounters had an audience of three or more people and in one in a hundred this involved more than ten people. Thus, an audience, although uncommon, is something the officer needs to know how to handle. Some younger officers seemed less threatened by an audience, possibly because their training has prepared them more specifically for such delicate situations. Half the encounters began in a street or other open space and a quarter of them continued there. Privacy was, therefore, not easily come by in these cases. Some of these street encounters were no more than requests for directions where there need be no concern about privacy, but for others there was something of a problem for the officer. Conversation with a policeman on the street may easily attract the curious because of its conspicuousness. Depending on the exact location there will be more and less conspicuous places to stand. It may be feasible to sit down on a bench, low wall, car bonnet or other object. On the other hand, without getting too deeply into matters of body language, if an officer wants to remain dominant in an encounter then he probably should remain standing. This maintains his physical presence in relation to others but it does keep him fairly conspicuous.

Three main ways were observed in which onlookers can be treated. First, the officer can try to ignore them. This may work for a while, but if they start to intrude into the dialogue, it cannot easily be sustained. Second, the officer can try to get rid of them. Asking them to 'move along please' in time honoured style may work, but it may well not. Single handed, the officer may simply be unable to turn his attention from his primary task and, if the crowd is at all curious or hostile it is unlikely to shift. Certainly if the request is made aggressively the officer is less likely to obtain compliance; he may do so, but he may equally just exacerbate the situation. The third, sometimes inevitable approach is to accept the situation and try to turn it to advantage by drawing onlookers — or individuals among them — into the encounter (Case 30). If they can be involved in some way they may then become allies of the officer. (The person he is primarily dealing with may do the same, of course, which can complicate matters.) At least three ways were seen of drawing onlookers into the encounter. First, to have them explain, or restate to one of the main participants what it is that the officer is trying to say to them. This can be useful where onlookers clearly have something more in common with the person than does the officer; in one case in mind young West Indians were able to explain something to an older West Indian who seemed not to understand the officer when he spoke directly to him. Other common factors may also be found. Second, third parties may act as translators where not just common understanding fails but there is an actual language barrier. Younger Asians sometimes are asked to do this when police need to communicate with their elders. Third, conciliation may be more acceptable to disputants if done by someone other than the police. These or other uses of onlookers may be appropriate to particular circumstances. Wherever onlookers are present, it can be in the officer's interests to use them constructively; they may have useful skills available, and their use brings the officer closer to them, reducing the chances that they will take against him and threaten his control of the encounter.

Apologies

Officers seemed to find it very threatening either to be wrong in any way or to be accused of behaving unjustly. Apologies for mistakes were often not offered when they might reasonably have been expected. Apology is difficult for a person whose job is, in a sense, to be right, and who is very concerned not to lose face with people he deals with in case they no longer respect him. But an apology need not put one at a disadvantage and officers need to realise that they will actually be respected more for admitting an honest mistake than they will for sticking to a line which the citizen is convinced is wrong. Errors of judgement are bound to be made sometimes, both initially, as when stopping and questioning someone, and in deciding if one was right to do so. But, where a genuine mistake has been made, an apology will gain rather than lose respect.

Another problem for the officer is where he is accused of something he does not feel he is guilty of, whether it be racist behaviour or a false accusation or suspicion. Such accusations are difficult to handle because they may or may not be justified, either objectively, or even in the eyes of the person making them. The officer needs to be very careful before reacting. Justified or not, accusations of bias strike at the officer's authority as an independent arbiter of justice and fair play, and question the assumption that he has authority to act in that role.

Formality

One of the most central human relations issues in patrol work is the question of how formally or informally an officer should behave. How friendly can he be without risk of losing public respect? In general, it seems clear that friendliness makes encounters run more smoothly, and that it is easier to begin on a friendly note and then become more severe if need be rather than to start off hostile and then try later to create an atmosphere of friendliness. The skilled officer can be relaxed and friendly and secure sufficient deference for his purposes at the same time. But, for the officer who is less sure of himself, the solution may seem to be a formality of manner at all times. Indeed, in just over half the encounters witnessed, officers were businesslike and civil in their manner towards the public, though they became slightly more friendly as the encounter progressed.

There may be occasions when a more formal manner is the most appropriate; friendliness may be seen as sarcasm, or as a trap to loosen the citizen's tongue and catch him off guard. Reliance on an overly formal manner when this is not needed seems undesirable, but each person and situation needs to be carefully judged for the degree of friendliness or formality appropriate.

Relaxing and taking tea

Even though the officer may decide that formality is not appropriate in a particular case, it may not be easy for him to strike a more relaxed note and get on friendly terms with the person he is dealing with. Mature and experienced officers generally handle this with greater ease, and there are a number of simple techniques which can be used. Central to this are acts which signify relaxation: sitting down, taking off the helmet, unbuttoning the coat or jacket are all clear signs of this kind. When the notebook has been in evidence prior to this point, putting it away fairly conspicuously serves to indicate that the next stage of the encounter is to be conducted on an 'off the record' or informal basis.

A popular technique (for various reasons) is the asking for or acceptance of, a cup of tea (Case 2); a generally accepted sign of sociability which, when engaged in by a police officer, indicates that all is sufficiently under control for him to be relaxing, rather than rushing to and fro, sending and receiving radio messages, looking for evidence or chasing suspects. (It also establishes a relationship of exchange and obligation between the officer and the citizen.) Although crime victims, at least, want the police to try to solve the crime or return their stolen property if they can they are equally, if not more, concerned about being treated pleasantly and sympathetically by the officer, as a way of returning to some state of normality.

Having a cup of tea (or similar actions) therefore reasures the public, but the officer must also consider whether he will need to become more formal again afterwards. Taking tea may relax the citizen, but it may also cause the officer to lower his guard and makes him less dominant. He may have to rebuild that dominance if he subsequently wants to secure some sort of compliance or action from the citizen and become more controlling.

Changing sides

In 7% of the encounters there was a clear shift in the apparent central nature of the encounter from the time of entry to the time of exit by the officer. This was often no more than a minor clarification but, in a few cases, there was a radical switch in the situation, so that the role of the citizen changed and the officer began to treat him as a suspect instead of a victim or vice versa. This is the most radical change which may occur, but there are others too: nuisance complainant to crime victim, person seeking advice to suspect, witness to suspect, and so on. These changes are an inevitable reflection of the ambiguity and confusion which pervades policing and do not necessarily take the officer totally unawares. One aspect of this is that many of the people he deals with he may regard as, first of all, 'police property' (Reiner, 1985) and only second as victims, suspects, etc.

But there are situations where the officer must adapt his manner to reflect the changed view which he finds himself taking. This can be especially difficult in the victim to offender role change.

Street enquiries

In more straightforward and non-problematic encounters, such as requests in the street for directions, deference and control are not immediately apparent as issues, but they are still negotiated in certain ways. By coming up to the officer and putting his question, the citizen is making clear an expectation that the officer possesses knowledge superior to his own, and thus puts himself in the officer's hands for the course of the brief conversation. Sometimes, though, the conversation becomes more extended: people ask directions at first, then start to talk to the officer about where they are going and what they will do when they arrive. They may start to ask his advice on what they should do: Should they buy the used car the person has advertised? What is their legal position in doing so? The conversation may, thus stray beyond direction-giving into other topics on which the officer is expected to have expertise or authority. In such cases he maintains some control of the encounter but, where more general topics are pursued it may become a totally discursive affair which the citizen seems inclined to pursue almost indefinitely. If the officer is on foot (and most such requests come to officers patrolling on foot) it can be difficult for him to end the conversation unless he makes a polite excuse and walks off somewhere different. He may have to calculate the trade-off between seeing the person as a time waster and the need to maintain good relations with the public.

On the other hand, it is possible that such an apparently random conversation may be leading up to something much more important about which the person feels unable to come directly to the point. This is also a familiar experience for doctors, who find patients talking about minor or even imagined symptoms as a way of leading up to some more serious concern (Pendleton *et al.*, 1984). Some encouragement may be needed by the doctor — or police officer — to bring these major concerns to the surface. Constant attention is, therefore, needed in order to distinguish conversations where something possibly important is waiting beneath the surface to be brought out into the open.

Teamwork

It is quite common for two officers to patrol together, and in half the observation sessions in the study the 'subject officer' was accompanied by another for all or part of the period of observation. Officers also came together in groups of two or more on some occasions and then dispersed again. One observer cannot observe all that two or more officers do and say as easily as with a single officer; if they go different ways during the course of an encounter, as can often happen, it becomes impossible to keep an adequate record. Observations, therefore, concentrated on what individual officers did, whether on lone patrol or as members of a team. But observers were often aware of the cooperation which was going on between officers and some limited comment is worth including.

Two officers can work together by sharing tasks at a practical level: they can each talk to one of the parties to a dispute (Case 30), one can go to the front of a building while the other checks the back, one can drive while the other observes, directs, makes notes or deals with the radio. They can perform similarly complementary roles when they interact with people. The 'hard' man and the 'soft' man who take turns to verbally 'work over' a suspect is almost a cliché, but variations on this theme were seen to work well for some pairs of officers observed. Rather than one being 'hard' and one 'soft', though, what sometimes happens is that one officer runs out of ideas or loses credibility with a person and the other officer then takes over and approaches the problem rather differently. This is not, of course, real teamwork, rather teamwork by accident, but it can be useful to be able to make an alternative approach when the first fails to work very well. Sometimes two officers clearly had varying views as to what the law required in a particular circumstance, or as to what action was appropriate. If officers are aware of this problem they should take care that no conflict of views becomes apparent to the public or their credibility could be severely compromised.

There is rather closer harmony when one officer does most of the talking so that the other can take notes or look around the area or the vehicle. Alternatively, both may take part in a conversation, pursuing the same theme in turn. How effectively this sort of teamwork is managed depends on the personalities of the two officers involved. Patrols are commonly shared with a succession of colleagues, so that the development of very close and symbiotic working relationships may be uncommon. Officers on a shift normally know which of their colleagues they work best with and develop ways of working with different individuals.

There are also dangers in having pairs of officers working together. One may be dominant and inhibit the contributions of the other. Two individuals may share a common fault and encourage each other to make this worse. In dealing with the public the worst thing which can probably happen is for two officers to act in concert to intimidate a person by, for example, bombarding him with questions too fast for him to answer, or by jointly invading his personal space so that he feels overwhelmed and threatened. It is, of course, a moot point as to how far such tactics can be justified in the pursuit of offenders. It is suggested that they cannot be justified in dealing with the great majority of public encounters where the person involved is almost certainly an innocent party.

(3) Form-filling and other constraints

Most students of policing come to the conclusion that organisational constraints and the work-group culture (often called the 'canteen culture') are both major influences on the behaviour and priorities of the police constable (Jones, 1980; Holdaway, 1983). This was certainly one of the clear conclusions to be drawn from the present study. It poses a real problem for the police trainer because unless what he teaches is endorsed by the organisation and its reward systems and by the canteen culture, then he will be facing an uphill struggle (Southgate, 1984).

The first thing to ask about organisational constraints is whether these constraints do actually affect how the constable behaves when he encounters the public or, indeed, if they determine whether he encounters them at all. And do the procedures, priorities, actions or words which the rules of the job require him to follow actually damage the quality of his relationship with the public?

In one sense the police constable is a mobile bureaucrat, required to record details of what he does for the benefit not only of himself but for members of the public, his superiors and the courts. There appeared to be some local variations in the amount and nature of form filling required of constables. But it was not the purpose of the study to comment on differences in force practice, and paperwork was certainly a significant part of the work all of those observed. One further point to note here is, of course, that the probationary constable is under much more pressure to make notes and produce a record of his work, for this is all part of the process by which he is being judged. At the end of his probation the danger is, of course, that he may either become very lax in his paperwork, doing the very minimum, or he may stick with the habits of the previous two years and keep on writing everything down. Either way there lie problems.

The need for a constable to fill in forms or make other written records can impinge upon his relationship with the public in at least two important ways. First, it may detract from the time he has available to do other things or even encourage him to avoid other work. For some officers observed in the study it could be anything up to an hour after the start of the shift before they had sorted out various reports and forms in the police station and actually gone out onto their beat. (Van Maanen (1984) has observed that, while the typical US patrolman seeks to get on to street patrol as soon as possible his British counterpart seems quite reluctant to leave the station. There may be various reasons for this, but it seems clear that at least one of these reasons is that he has so much paperwork to cope with.) In one instance constables working from a vehicle were reluctant to get back into the car after attending an incident until they had finished their paperwork, because if they did they might get sent somewhere else immediately and have to do it later.

The very act by a policeman of taking out his notebook and writing down information — a name and address or other items — has always signified a rather serious step to a member of the public. It indicates that the constable has decided to take the matter seriously, that a person has overstepped some limit of the law, or that further action may follow with repercussions of an unknown, possibly serious nature. Just how a person feels when the notebook or form appears will depend broadly on whether that person is a complainant/victim or a suspect. In general, a complainant will feel that his problem is now being taken seriously, while a suspect is more likely to see himself getting deeper into trouble when the officer starts to make a permanent record.

For a victim or complainant the constable's act of writing can be reassuring, but it can also lead to embarrassing silences in the conversation or give the appearance that the officer is not listening properly to what the person is telling him; this in turn may cause ill feeling which could easily be avoided (Case 10). Officers were observed who overcame some of these difficulties by going twice through the complainant's story; the first time they listened and gave all their attention to the person. Then they went through it again writing as they went and clarifying points in the story. This has the advantage of checking things which at second telling may not seem so clear as at first, it displays thoroughness on the officer's part, and it gives him the chance to pay more initial attention to the person; apart from reassuring them it can also give the officer a chance to look at the person while they tell their tale to pick up non-verbal cues from their behaviour.

If the constable does not write much while with the complainant, the latter may conclude that his problem is not being taken seriously. The optimum course of action therefore seems to be for the officer to write as little as possible initially, and to leave as much as possible until later but to offer some assurance that he will be making such a record and taking other further actions. Clearly a balance has to be struck. If the officer is overburdened with forms and records to be made he may alienate the public by his apparent reluctance to listen to and look directly at them. But if he makes no or too little record then valuable information may get forgotten or overlooked and the public may think that he is not taking their problem seriously because he has not written it all down.

Many officers fear that the implementation of the Police and Criminal Evidence Act will increase their paperwork load. If this proves to be the case it seems likely that some officers will cope with it by avoiding some of the things which involve extra paperwork for them. Alternatively, they may do the extra paperwork at the expense of contact with the public. The evidence from the observations suggested that both these things may happen.

Summary

This chapter has considered a number of the human relations issues which arise during the middle stages of an encounter. These were seen as falling under two main headings: respect for people's feelings and control and deference. A wide range of issues arose under each of these, all of which were seen by observers to have some bearing upon the quality of relations between police and public. In themselves, some seem more trivial than others but, on a cumulative basis their impact can be considerable, and the purpose in presenting them in this way is to argue for a greater recognition of this by police officers. Also included in this chapter has been a discussion of how the demands for paperwork from the constable can impinge on the way the job gets done.

6 Leaving the encounter

This chapter looks at how encounters come to an end and how constables resolve the issues they raise.

Only one encounter in a hundred took more than an hour to complete; 10% of them took between 30 and 60 minutes; 14% took from 15 to 30 minutes; 28% took from 5 to 15 minutes; 30% took from 1 to 5 minutes; and 17% took under one minute.

They were resolved by the officer in various ways (Table 6:1). In many cases – almost half, in fact – all that was involved was some 'closing' remark rather than any specific decision or action. Only one in a hundred of all encounters seen were concluded with a sarcastic or hostile remark from the officer; in others it was either neutral or, most commonly, friendly in tone.

Some kind of formal legal action – such as an arrest or making a report – was taken in one encounter in six, most commonly for theft and burglary reports. One encounter in five ended with 'informal' enforcement, such as a traffic warning or a promise or threat that some police action might be taken at a future time; this happened most where reports of vandalism were involved, and also in disturbances and stops. One in fourteen encounters ended with the officer offering some kind of advice, arbitration or referral; most often in emergencies and calls for assistance, assault reports and disturbances. One in twenty involved physical or medical assistance, especially in emergencies and calls for assistance. In three per cent of encounters people were persuaded they could cope with the problem themselves, and one percent were told specifically that this was not a police matter; both these last two were seen most in disturbances.

Police clearly do a wide variety of things other than enforce the law. What they do may be determined by a number of factors, but without knowing precisely what considerations were being weighed in the officer's mind, it is difficult to say which of these was most influential in any given decision. One of these will be the nature of the contact and what the law has to say about dealing with such issues, but it is also likely that the demeanour of the citizen sometimes plays a significant part. Observers noted cases where officers enforced the law 'by the book' in response to difficult or hostile people, whereas they applied discretion to offenders of a similar kind who were more amenable. As an indicator of this it can be noted that some 'official' law enforcement action was taken in 22% of encounters where the citizen was civil in the closing stage, 11% where he was friendly, only 5% where he showed particular deference to the officer, but in 45% of encounters where he was rude or hostile.

Table 6:1   **Resolution of encounters**

Resolution	Subject of encounter									All
	Emergency	Theft	Burglary	Assault	Vandalism/damage	Disturbances	Information from public	Police initiated	Casual/social	
	%	%	%	%	%	%	%	%	%	%
Formal enforcement	16	47	46	31	33	4	3	12	—	17
Informal enforcement	8	12	21	21	38	27	8	27	—	19
Physical help	29	10	—	7	5	3	—	3	—	5
Advise or refer	17	—	6	17	5	21	3	1	4	7
Persuaded no problem	2	3	4	10	8	14	1	—	—	3
Persuaded not police matter	—	3	1	—	3	5	1	1	—	1
Closing remark	28	24	22	14	8	26	83	55	96	48
n =	83	59	109	29	39	102	89	235	110	855

(N.I./unclear = 126)

48

Where the person involved has been guilty of some offence he may need some explanation both of legal procedures and of the rationale of the law, and of the likely course of events. Particularly for minor offenders who feel that what they have done is not an offence or that it merits no police action, a convincing explanation from the officer can help to reduce resentment at the action he takes and possibly help prevent future offending.

The termination of any encounter with someone accused of an offence poses its own problems. It is probably unrealistic to think that all those encountering the police can be sent on their way happy; if they have been caught in breach of the law they may be unhappy however nice to them the officer is. What is important is that hostility and ill feeling are kept to a minimum. One way to do this is to avoid conflict from becoming personalised; this may be achieved if officers can present themselves as impartial arbiters of the law. At the same time, though they need to avoid the impresssion of 'going by the book' in a completely arbitrary and unimaginative way, and need to exercise discretion for minor offences where enforcement would achieve nothing.

One way in which honour can be satisfied on both sides is where some kind of 'natural justice' appears to have been done. Where an offender has already suffered in some way because of his law breaking, the officer may feel that he has been punished sufficiently without any further official legal action taking place. With some minor offences it may even be that being stopped and reprimanded by the officer has itself been an adequate punishment. For his part, the offender will be relieved not to be subjected to legal actions, and pleased with the officer for not causing this to happen. If the officer insists on 'going by the book' in such circumstances the offender may feel he has been overly punished and become resentful, rather than recognising that he did wrong and should expect some punishment.

In looking at the way problems of order maintenance and social service are dealt with, there are two basic conceptions of police work to be considered; one which sees the police task as dealing with problems in a short term view with no pretence of getting to grips with the underlying issues, and one which sees it as trying to gain at least some understanding of those underlying issues, with a view to doing something about them. Although, to the layman, the latter seems much more satisfactory, there is a perfectly sound case for the 'first aid' approach because, so often, there is little the police can do about the real problem even if they do understand it. The way that domestic – and other – disputes are treated by constables provides a prime illustration of this issue.

Police recruits on the Initial Training Course have traditionally been taught that the object of police attendance at the scene of a domestic dispute is to restore the peace. The lesson notes contain perfectly sound advice such as the need to remain calm and patient, appear sensitive to problems, and to refer parties to "suitable services or agencies such as social services, local authority, race relation board, solicitor and marriage guidance council" (Home Office, 1983). In practice, however, what can so easily happen is that the police arrive, stop any violence currently taking place, listen to the parties, decide there is no offence they can take action on and that things are calm for the moment, say "see your solicitor" and leave (Case 6). To the observers it so often seemed that this approach failed to get to grips with the fundamental problems in people's lives, and ignored the facts that many of those involved probably did not know how to contact a solicitor and thought they could not afford to do so in any case.

In principle, mechanisms exist by which police can make referrals to other agencies. But there was only limited evidence of this happening. Taking all types of disputes and disturbances together (a total of 102 during the observations) only one in five were dealt with by a referral. The rest were dealt with by means of 'informal' law enforcement such as moralising or threatening future action (one in ten), by telling people to sort it out themselves (one in five), or simply with some fairly non-committal remark like 'Well I'll be off now then' (one in four). In only four cases was an arrest made or even threatened.

There appeared to be various reasons why officers were reluctant to attempt referrals (see also Ekblom, 1986). One is the generally low opinion which police officers have of social workers (as individuals rather than necessarily as an institutional body), seeing them as left-wing, anti-police trouble makers (Reiner, 1985). Some complained of the delays they felt such referrals could produce. There is also a kind of professional pride which prevents officers from turning to other professionals to help them solve problems, despite the fact that they often feel that these problems are not police matters in any case. Any such involvement may be seen as a threat to the perceived autonomy of the police (Punch, 1979). The situation is, of course, self-perpetuating in that the less inter-professional contact which takes place in this way, the less understanding there is of how this could be helpful and the less likely it is that an effective service will be provided.

Pride of this kind also works against the referral of problems – about disputes or any other matters – to an officer's superiors. The fear is that this shows weakness and lack of skill at one's job which one ought to possess, and that revealing this weakness will result in unfavourable reports and reduced promotion chances.

Sometimes referral does not take place because officers genuinely do not understand the situation, but it may simply be that they know from experience that however hard they try they are unlikely to solve the problem. As noted in the previous chapter, it seems unlikely that a police officer alone can achieve any very effective resolution of a husband-wife dispute, and some research suggests that the simplest and most effective way (in terms of reducing repeat calls to the police) to resolve the situation may be to arrest the husband. Some officers were reluctant to make arrests in such circumstances on the grounds that a wife's complaint might then be withdrawn.

Whatever they do subsequently though, police officers still have to make the initial contact, and need to be trained to understand problems in enough depth so that they know what immediate action to take and when to refer. What they concentrate on at the moment is to see whether there has been any kind of offence committed. If there has this provides them with a focus for further action, and resolution of the encounter will consist largely of transactions relating to this offence. Where there is no offence apparent to the constable what so often happens is that he seeks to quieten down the disputants and make as quick an exit as possible. He knows that he is unlikely to achieve anything lasting by staying around talking for long periods, so he does not usually bother to do so. What has happened in such cases is that the constable has failed to agree the problem with the citizen because there was no legal problem he could focus on. There may well be some civil dispute to be dealt with but he does not see that as a matter for himself and opts out of the situation by saying "see your solicitor".

Another problematic remark heard in dispute cases and others was to the effect that an assault was 'only' a common assault. While such a statement may be legally true the distinction between this and more serious assaults is likely to be a matter of irrelevance to a victim. Particularly if prefixed by 'only' such a reference can be distressing and insulting, implying that the matter is too trivial to take note of. This can actually be what the officer does mean, but it certainly should not be put so bluntly.

Given the undoubted talking and negotiating skills which some officers have, why do they not apply them more effectively to solving disputes? One possible reason is that however well they might be able to negotiate the dispute in an immediate sense, officers know that there is inadequate organisational backup at the end of the day to which they can refer people for continuing help. This is not helped by the lack of faith which most officers have in social workers, so that they avoid dealing with them wherever possible. Knowing that anything they themselves can achieve will be short lived without long term support, it is little wonder that so many officers seem to deal with domestic problems in a cursory and insensitive manner.

Where the officer was originally called by a complainant, he has to decide at some point whether there is any action he can take and is willing to take, or whether there is anything the complainant himself can do. In either case, the officer needs to be able to explain in a realistic way just what will be involved in taking the matter further, whether through the criminal justice system or other channels. Clear explanation will be necessary, and it must not be assumed that the citizen has the same grasp of legal institutions and procedures as the officer does or, indeed, that he has any grasp at all. There must, therefore, be more than the "see your solicitor" type of remark if the officer is to carry any credibility or to be of much help. Many people have no idea of how to contact a solicitor, never mind having one 'on tap' as the advice seems to assume. Moreover, it can seem like a very major step to take involving them in costly and delayed proceedings when what they really want is some immediate help and resolution.

Summary

Many police-public encounters ended with little more than some verbal comment from the officer. This reflects the facts that (a) many of them are essentially casual

51

conversations rather than problems as such to be dealt with, and (b) many problems which are brought to the police cannot actually be dealt with in any other way. But, whichever the explanation, it is clear that police constables must be effective talkers. While bad feelings can be created by the way an officer enforces the law, they can also arise when there is no law to enforce. If there is an ambiguous situation where he does not know what to do for the best, or one where the citizen expects there to be a legal solution where none exists, then resentment and misunderstanding can ensue. So often members of the public bring a problem to the police only to find that they cannot or will not solve it for them. If they are not to go away disappointed and resentful, then effort is needed from the constable to ensure that (a) he does do as much as he can, or refers the problem to someone who could do something, or (b) he helps the person to understand why it is that their problem cannot be solved by the police.

7 Conclusions

This study has looked at police encounters with the public to examine the ways in which they are problematic and ambiguous and in which they are difficult for the patrol officer to resolve. It has tried to illustrate the human relations issues raised for both parties and to ask, especially, what the uniformed officer can do about them. The aim has not been to provide clear cut answers or to develop ideal models of behaviour, but to raise questions which training might consider. Value judgements about police behaviour have been made, but these are offered primarily as ideas or hypotheses for consideration rather than as definitive conclusions. The practical purpose has been to inject these ideas into the training process, along with supporting material, which trainers can use as they see fit. It is hoped that, as a whole, the report will provide issues for discussion plus material for case studies, role play exercises and videos. It is also hoped that it will be a spur to further investigations and to a generally more questioning approach to how relations with individual members of the public should be handled.

The research was not designed primarily to study the distribution of police time between various types of activity; rather, its purpose was to look at as many encounters as possible in a qualitative manner. In pursuing this objective, however, it did provide some interesting quantitative material. This material provides a picture of the calls the officers attended, and of the other encounters they had with the public while they were actually out on street patrol. (This is not the same as a description of how time is divided throughout a typical eight hour shift, which includes varying periods of time on police premises or performing tasks which do not involve direct contact with the public.) As with so many research studies, there is the question of how representative a picture the sampled police divisions provided. This picture may vary in points of detail, but it seems likely that the events and problems described would be familiar to officers in urban forces other than those studied. With these reservations, there are a number of observations to be made about the overall pattern of police-public contact, many of them confirming the findings of previous studies.

Police patrol is, for most of the time, a quite mundane and undramatic activity. This is due largely to the mundane nature of the calls which the public make on the police, but it may also result from the manner in which officers conduct themselves. The amounts of hostility or conflict which the study found were small; with few exceptions, encounters were conducted in normal, not raised, voices, and the participants were civil, or even friendly, rather than rude to each other and, overall, there was a slight increase in the friendliness as encounters proceeded. It is conceivable that hostility was sometimes reduced by the presence of observers, but there was little evidence of this.

Despite the above comments, there were a minority of contacts where there was some degree of hostility. This may sometimes be unavoidable; policing by its very nature involves people being asked questions they do not want to answer and made to do things they do not want to do. But even these more 'adversarial' situations can be handled in better and worse ways. And there were a great many more occasions when, although no serious conflict arose, matters were handled less well than they need have been. The bulk of the study has been concerned with such matters, and has discussed the sources of such problems. This it has done not simply by reference to traditional categories such as domestic disputes, foot stops, robberies etc, or to different groups of the population (motorists, young men, ethnic minorities etc), but to categories of human relations problem, such as prior expectations, sensitivity to feelings, deference, and agreeing the purpose of the encounter.

Traffic policing

One of the most common types of encounter observed arose from the stopping of a vehicle. Evidence from other studies confirms how common this is for drivers. Given the massive growth in vehicle ownership and use in recent decades, vehicle stops provide the context for a very large proportion of police-public contacts, and there are unique features of these contacts which can cause difficulties.

There are distinctive ways in which vehicle-centred encounters begin which emphasise that the police officer is taking control of the public and ordering their actions. This in itself can create hostilities and tensions if the officer behaves aggressively or the citizen reacts in an uncooperative manner. The stop in itself carries a clear implied suspicion of some guilt, and a major ambiguity lies in whether the suspicion is of a driving offence, a vehicle offence, a criminal offence, or none of these. The officer is aware of these doubts on the part of the driver and is in a powerful position if he cares to exploit it. There are some easy ways for him to do this because, until he actually declares himself satisfied to the contrary, the citizen knows that he may be in trouble if he does not cooperate. By delaying this declaration, for example, tension can be created which, in a short term view may serve the officer's purpose but in the long term can easily go towards a build up of generalised resentment against the police.

The study included a number of stops of drivers by police in panda cars, but did not deal with traffic patrols as such; this is one area of police work which remains relatively poorly understood. Apart from the human relations problems involved, there are important questions to be asked about its resource costs and its effectiveness, and all these issues would repay further study.

Referrals

Many people live their lives in a state of continual crisis or near crisis. For others this may be less so but they still have moments of emergency. At these moments of crisis and emergency the police become involved. The question then is whether the police should try to get to grips with the underlying problems and help people to solve them or to go to someone who may be able to help. What officers more often do is to see whether there are any clear breaches of the law, deal with them if there are, and then leave as soon as possible. Sometimes they tell people to "see your solicitor", a singularly unhelpful piece of advice to many of those receiving it. Most police officers would probably say that realistically this is all they can achieve and, within the present limitations of their job, this may well be the case.

Organisational factors

All encounters take place within a social, legal, physical and organisational context. The study was concerned primarily with the first, with reference to the other three, but it very soon became apparent how influential the organisational context was. Procedural and organisational constraints were often so dominant as to receive much more attention from the constable than questions of public relations, and there were various ways in which such factors affected behaviour.

First, there is a general concern to be seen by one's supervisor to be doing what is regarded as a good job. As the Metropolitan Police Commissioner's report for 1984 (Home Office, 1985) notes, the pressure on the young constable to produce 'figures' in order to prove his worth is now much less than it once was, but it will take some time to vanish completely, having been so central to the police ethic for so long. The study found some evidence of this kind of concern, though mostly among probationers, who did still feel they were required to make more scrupulous paper records than older officers. This concern was reflected both in the time and trouble which officers gave to different issues, and in the paper records they actually kept as they went about their work. The main problem here is the intrusiveness of the required form filling resulting, in some cases, in embarrassment, loss of rapport with the public, and public misunderstanding about subsequent actions to be taken. The codification of procedures represented by the Police and Criminal Evidence Act indicates a need for alertness to these problems; it is vital for the constable to be aware of the impact which form filling – like all his other actions – can have upon his communication with the public and the trust they accord him.

A second organisational factor which impinges upon the nature and quality of encounters is the radio control system. Although the majority of encounters were initiated by the public, these requests were mostly conveyed to the officer on the beat through the radio control system. This meant that the patrol constable was normally heavily dependent for information about the call upon what the controller told him. This information, for various reasons, is often very inadequate, so that the constable frequently arrived at a call poorly informed as to what he was going into. In extreme cases this could put him in danger; far more often it meant that the conversation got off on the wrong foot, either because the officer did not know the facts which he ought to have known, or because in order to compensate for lack of information he sometimes created expectations based on hearsay, past experience, or stereotyping. Thus, he could begin with largely false expectations about the people, events or circumstances with which he was dealing, or he might try to bluff his way until more information emerged. As systems of graded response are developed there should be less pressure to rush every call as soon as possible. It is to be hoped that some of this extra time can be used for the attending officer to become as well informed as he can about the problem and the people involved before he actually arrives at the scene of a call.

A third organisational problem is the way in which the occupational culture favours a law enforcement approach to policing over a broader social problem-solving approach. This in turn leads to stereotyping and the labelling of people in terms of the way they impinge upon the job of law enforcement or detract from its pursuit with their demands for service on more 'trivial' matters. This, and all other studies of police-public contact, make it clear that the public do not limit their demands to matters falling within the criminal law or, indeed, the law as a whole. The role of the police as originally defined is not, in fact, a narrow one, but many police officers do try to make it so thereby denying the facts of life of their occupation. Current police management initiatives which involve setting out goals and objectives can only be helpful in this context, by defining for the patrol officer where his priorities should lie, not only in law enforcement but in other areas of the job also.

A fourth area of concern about organisational factors is the lack of coordination and backup for dealing with disputes and other crises which people suffer. One reason that officers deal so superficially with some such problems is simply that they do not have agencies or individuals they can turn to for help, or that they do not know about them even when they do exist. The antipathy between police officers and social workers is no secret, and each side sees good reason for criticising the other. If better understanding and more cooperation are to be achieved then perhaps ways should be found to formalise working relationships between the two. The police are proud of the fact that they provide what, in many places, is the only 24 hour a day crisis service. But they cannot simply leave it at that if they are to provide a service which achieves anything useful.

Fifthly, there are a range of sometimes very minor constraints and influences upon the way officers behave which could be minimised or reduced through better management and supervision. The issuing of gloves which are not too tight is one example. This may seem totally trivial, but police officers suggest that this is quite a common practice and that they almost unconsciously respond by punching one hand with another to try and stretch them. But, to the outsider, this looks like an aggressive gesture. Supervisors should be alert for any such minor problems which could detract from the quality of relations with the public.

The general point about these organisational considerations is quite simple; it is that training alone is not enough. If those in the police organisation – or any other large organisation – are to be taught to behave in certain ways, then the lessons of training need to be reinforced by the work environment. This includes supervisory standards, rewards and sanctions, peer values and work procedures.

Training

Like other people, police officers do their job within, on the one hand, the constraints of their own capabilities and, on the other hand, the limitations which circumstances and the organisation place upon them. It is easy to criticise instances of police insensitivity and to suggest that the police do not tackle the real problems people have; more or better training seems like one easy remedy for these shortcomings. But most police officers are not professional sociologists or psychologists, although some may develop considerable skills in these areas at a practical level during the course of their careers. One must, therefore, consider very carefully just how sophisticated training should become in this direction. In doing this one arrives again at the question of what the police are supposed to be doing. The police patrol function could, theoretically, be reconceptualised as primarily a job of social work, and recent years have seen no shortage of research evidence which can be used to argue such a case. But if such a major shift took place in the official definition of the police officer's job, then the police service might have to recruit people with rather different backgrounds and interests than at present. In particular, it might be necessary to attract people with an aptitude for counselling and an understanding of social problems, including some with rather stronger academic backgrounds, capable of thinking at some depth about society and its problems. At present this level of thinking may be found within senior police management circles, but it is not something which is routinely encouraged among junior ranks.

This study was conceived as a contribution to police training, and its primary purpose was to gather material for use in training rather than to explore teaching strategies. But there are two central messages for training which must accompany both the report and the case study material. The first message is that it is neither possible nor desirable to think of human relations training as training in how to manipulate people, tempting though this propect must sometimes seem to the police officer faced with various forms of chaos. "People handling' skills can certainly be used in policing but any 'game' needs two to play, and an officer can only succeed so far in manipulating a person if that person does not choose to be manipulated. In any case, there are so many facets to human interaction that few officers are likely to achieve total mastery of them. The second message is that what training needs is more questions and fewer answers. This is a proposition which it is difficult for a large hierarchically structured organisation like the police to accept.

For reasons of law, civil rights, efficiency and so on there are strong pressures for standardisation of police behaviour and, thus, of police training. For the most part this is commendable, but there are very many occasions in policing when the exercise of discretion and of personal initiative may be needed to cope with a problem for which a standard set of rules cannot hope to be adequate. This personal initiative may be needed at all levels of decision making and in many different circumstances. It may involve decisions for the constable about how and when to arrive at a certain call, what to say at certain points in a conversation, what tactical choices to pursue in handling a problem, or how to resolve matters and leave. In the interests of consistency and fairness it might be desirable to reduce to an absolute minimum the need for individual initiative and choice, but there are limits to how far this is possible. (If there were not and every decision and choice could be programmed, there would be great losses in job satisfaction and morale.)

Some situations are predictable or easy to deal with and some are difficult or problematic. Training has to prepare officers to be able to identify which of these situations they are facing and to react accordingly, whether this means behaving in some very standardised way or whether it means using considerable imagination and creativity. The first priority, then, is that officers should be able to recognise the various dimensions of different situations. What they must be able to do is to go further than simply asking themselves what piece of law does or does not apply, but to ask how they can use the law or other resource to deal with the problem they find, and how to do this in a sensitive and helpful manner. Training for this can be given, but it is difficult to give well, difficult to absorb and often difficult to apply. What must also be done is to ensure that as many practical steps as possible are taken to make the constable's job easier, by removing obstacles to good relations between him and the public.

In almost any organisation, and certainly in the police service, changes in working methods are unlikely to be achieved through training alone. Unless training is seen by the trainees as having the endorsement of the organisation it will probably not be worth their while to take the trouble to learn and apply the lessons. Endorsement is needed from all levels but particularly from those to whom the trainees are most directly and frequently answerable in their day to day work.The reward system of the organisation should reflect the values and standards which the training seeks to impart; if people know that they are more likely to be promoted or to be better paid, or to get pleasanter assigments if they do certain things in certain ways, then it is much more likely that those things will actually get done in those ways. The way to achieve this sort of response will involve more than simply rewarding certain behaviour, but will also require that the structure of the organisation and of its work should be changed in such a way that particular practices are made easier to adopt. For no amount of training or praise and reward can get something done in a certain way if there are other things about the work environment which make it difficult for that to happen.

Some human relations problems result not from the inadequacies of individuals, but from the rules, procedures and structures within which they have to work. By its very nature, policing deals with many existing problems of this kind, and also produces others; however 'well' an officer behaves the arrest of a person for an offence involves something of a 'human relations problem', and there is no way this can be changed. But there are some things which officers have to do which cause problems which might possibly be avoided by redesigning procedures rather than training people to behave differently.

Appendix 1: Case studies

Introduction

The following pages contain descriptions of some of the events which were witnessed by observers in this study. All references to real names, places or other clues to the identity of police officers or members of the public have, of course, been removed or changed, and some editing has been done so as to make the accounts as clear as possible. But the dialogues and descriptions remain essentially the same as when they were first written down by the observers at the time of the events described or shortly after.

Each study consists of a script of the dialogue and an account (mainly factual, but with some commentary – shown in italics – from the observer) of what took place from the time the officer first approached or was approached by the member(s) of the public involved, or from when he arrived at the address to which he had been sent. It finishes at the point where they parted company or, in rare cases, when they went into a police station.

Each account includes the more important parts of the dialogue which took place. 'Important' may seem a very subjective word here but, in most cases, all that is meant is that very mundane or repetitive parts of dialogue are excluded. The accounts vary in length, just as the encounters themselves did. Some very lengthy descriptions have been included in order to give of the full flavour of some of the complexities with which officers are confronted. Others can be described much more briefly.

Only about three per cent of all the encounters observed have been included here (though others could be made available to trainers). In making this selection, similar principles have been followed to those described in the main text relating to the selection of human relations problems for discussion. Thus, to some extent, the examples represent the frequency of certain types of encounter. But many of the commoner encounters seemed to raise few problems; the dialogue was mundane, they were non-problematic for the officer and seemed to be so for the public also. Weight has also been given, therefore, to the need for cases where the officer faced a dilemma or a state of confusion. If more negative than positive examples seem to be included, this is because (a) there is often more to be learned from the negative ones and (b) well handled encounters are often briefer than badly handled ones and provide less material to describe and discuss.

Using the case studies

The case studies can be read and used in various ways. First, they are an accompaniment to the main text in that they provide illustrations of some of the issues raised there. (References to case numbers are given in the text.) More generally, they provide a picture of the things which police officers on patrol actually do, and the ways in which the police and public talk to each other. For the non-police reader they provide insights into the world of police patrol and, even for the experienced police officer they may, hopefully, still provide some new insights into police work, looked at from the perspective of a detatched outsider.

Their second purpose is as material for police trainers. It is for trainers to decide just how they will use the accounts, but there are two obvious ways of doing this. They can be used as discussion material, with trainees – under the guidance of the trainer – reading them and considering the issues they raise, alternative courses of action for the constable involved and so on. The other, related, way of using them is as scripts for role playing exercises. To this end as much dialogue as possible has been included, and some preference has been given in selection to those cases which contain a maximum of dialogue. Preference has also been given to encounters where members of ethnic minorities were involved because, as mentioned earlier in the report, there is a particular interest in some quarters in data of this kind.

It is suggested that the following minimum list of questions be raised for each case study considered:

i. How was this encounter initiated?

ii. What information was available to the constable prior to the encounter?

iii. What do you think the officer was expecting as he approached the encounter?

iv. What seemed to be the central issue when the officer first arrived?

v. Was it mainly a legal problem, a human relations problem, or some other sort of problem?

vi. What human relations problems did the officer have to confront?

vii. To what extent were these inherent in the situation and to what extent did they arise during the encounter? (For example, a domestic dispute is largely a human relations problem in itself, whereas driving without a licence is a legal matter, but human relations problems may arise from the way the officer and the driver speak to each other.)

viii. If they arose during the encounter how did this happen, who was responsible and what could the officer have done to avoid or overcome them?

ix. What did the officer do to deal with the various problems in the encounter, however they arose?

x. What examples of good and bad practice would you identify in this encounter?

For the sake of simplicity in labelling, each of the following cases is headed according to the main legal or other issue involved. Some indication is also given as to the sort of human relations issues illustrated, and where ethnic minorities were involved in this is also shown.

Reason for encounter: Page

1. **Burglary**   63
Friendly officer.

2. **Racial harassment**   64
Asians – tea – politeness.

3. **Criminal damage**   65
W Indian youth wrongly suspected – racist language.

4. **Criminal damage**   67
W Indian – complaints of delay – officer annoyed – anti-black
comments later.

5. **Burglary**   69
W Indian victim – very agitated – complaints of delay.

6. **Domestic dispute**   71
Asians – racist joke on setting off – slow response – no
real resolution.

7. **Delivering news of an arrest**   73
Friendly officer – but poorly informed on case.

8. **Motorcycle offences**   73
Insolent youth.

9. **Stolen road signs**   75
Some embarrassment – arrest.

10. **Burglary**   76
Lot of paperwork – embarrassing silences – no conversation.

11. **Racial harassment/assault**   77
Harassment not investigated – insolent young women – PC calm.

12. **Vehicle stop**   79
W Indian – breathalyser – lack of deference – escalation – arrest.

13. **Vehicle stop**   81
Delays – paperwork – lack of conversation.

14. Burglary   82
W Indians – very long and confusing for PC – upset people –
accusations of discrimination.

15. Shoplifting/drunk   90
Drunk making a disturbance – struggle – arrest.

16. Assault   91
Prostitutes – sarcasm to PC – they better informed than he? – ambiguity
for PC.

17. Indecency   93
Embarrassment – need for privacy.

18. Foot stop   96
Two W Indian boys running – PC ignorant of local schools.

19. Dispute at shop   98
Asians – PC first says 'see solicitor' then acts when finds local villain
involved.

20. Vehicle stop   100
W Indian – cross with PC – delay – PC sarcastic – later comments
about 'coloureds'.

21. Foot stop   101
W Indian youth with bag – resents police stops – officer sarcastic.

22. Foot stop   102
W Indian youth – cooperates, so PC does not prolong encounter.

23. Vehicle stops (2)   103
Contrasts two identical situations. Both drivers polite, but one (W Indian)
let go with warning by friendly officer; other reported by PC who 'loves'
traffic offences – delay – paperwork.

24. Domestic dispute   107
Woman and homosexual – they embarrassed – officer in 'chairman'
role – helpful.

25. Squatters/drugs   108
Cavalier PC attitude – youth defiant and abusive – PC aggressive –
arrest.

26. Domestic dispute   110
W Indian – PC in 'chairman' role – helpful – respects privacy –
possibly favours man?

27. Landlord-tenant dispute   113
W Indian – long and confused – PC accused of discrimination – later
says can't get through to W Indians.

28. Foot stop   119
W Indian – PC shouting out of car – resentment develops – more
friendly conclusion.

29. Vehicle stop   121
Some confusion about driver's identity – civil.

30. Betting shop disturbance   123
Teamwork by PCs – onlookers used to help explain.

31. Delivering a summons   127
Lack of privacy.

1. Burglary

A WPC was on car patrol accompanied by a male PC driver.

Before leaving the police station she was told to deal with a 'break-in'. It was 6.15 pm on arrival. The door was opened by a twenty year old woman.

WPC: "Hello, called the police?"

Woman: "Yes, you have to laugh, it must've happened last night. I came down to go to the loo and the back had been broken into. The back door was open! They've done the meters too."

The WPC went to the back of the house to investigate. There was a broken window in the bathroom and the back door was very insecure. Now the WPC went out into the garden, where she noticed that a coal bunker had provided the burglar with an easy step up to the bathroom window. She returned to the house and the young woman introduced her to her mother to whom the constable directed most of her questions.

WPC: "Now I'm going to ask a question you'll like. When were you born?"

The woman laughed and gave her date of birth. The WPC started to fill in the crime report chatting at the same time. She made some jokes and managed to raise some smiles from the victims.

WPC: "Were you born here?"

Woman 2: "No, in —."

WPC: "What made you move here then?"

The woman laughed. All this time, a little boy, presumably the young woman's son, had been looking at the WPC with a big grin. Now, the young woman told the WPC:

Woman: "He likes the police."

WPC: (To little boy) "Do you want to come with us?"

The little boy laughed at her question and pretended to hit her leg. Now it was the constable's turn to laugh. She completed the rest of the report and before leaving, gave the woman advice about how to pay back the electricity board the money which had been stolen from the meter. She told her that the social services would help her, and also advised her to get a quarterly bill, so as not to risk her meter money being stolen again.

The woman asked a bit frightened:

Woman 2: "Do you think they'll come back?"

WPC: "No, lightning doesn't strike twice often, not two nights in a row anyway!"

The woman thanked her and she left saying:

"Take care."

The WPC's approach made for a very natural and easy-going encounter.

2. Racial harassment

A PC (aged 33) was on patrol alone in a panda car. At 7.15 pm he went to pay a second visit to a Pakistani family that had been harassed by some youths the previous day. The youths had been throwing snowballs at their window and one of them had jumped on the bonnet of their car. They had also called them "paki bastards". The constable had asked them to try to find out the names of the youths and the reason for his present call was to ask them whether they now knew the youths' names.

On arrival, an Asian man opened the door and said in a friendly manner:

Man: "Hello."

His wife was standing at the end of the hall and seeing the constable shouted:

Woman: "What have you done to the weather?"

64

They all went into the sitting room where the couple's 2 sons were sitting.

PC: "Did you manage to get the names of the persons responsible?"

Man: "Yes . . . I am worried about my car."

PC: "So what you want me to do is to see these lads' parents and tell them what's happened."

Man: "Yes."

PC: "We've had a lot of trouble with people throwing snowballs, it may not be because you're Asian, but if they're calling you names, it's upsetting you and that's another thing."

The officer accepted the offer of a cup of tea and made polite conversation with the adults, who seemed very pleased that he was spending some time with them.

The constable left to make enquiries at an address where the youth that had been jumping on the car supposedly lived. As it happened, the youth was not in and the observer was not able to follow the enquiries made by the constable subsequently.

On the way to the youth's home the constable said to the observer:

PC: "Really, they haven't done anything which should involve the police (the car had not been damaged), but who else have they (the Asians) got to turn to?"

3 Criminal damage

It was a very cold evening with thick snow on the ground.

A WPC (aged 28) was patrolling alone in a panda car at about 9.15 pm when she noticed three youths walking very slowly down a side road off a dual carriage way. There were two white youths on one side of the road and a black youth on the other. She passed them slowly and then drove to the end of the road, where she turned round. As there was a closed petrol station on the corner of the dual carriageway and the side street, she thought the youths may have been up to no good. She decided to stop at the petrol station to check nothing was amiss.

She examined the petrol station's office and found a small crack on the window, but it looked old. While she was doing this an eighteen year old white man approached her saying:

Man: "Three white lads just put the window in on the shop over the road."

WPC: "Do you mind coming in the car to see if you can spot them?"

The man got into the police car and the WPC drove down the side road, where she had previously seen three youths. The two white youths had disappeared, but the black youth was still walking down the road. Stopping the car the WPC shouted to the black youth:

WPC: "Hold on a minute."

Then she got out of the car and approached him.

WPC: "Where've you been?"

Youth: "Round friends."

WPC: "Where?"

The youth gave her an address.

WPC: "Where are you going?"

Youth: "Home."

WPC: "Have you been in trouble with the law before?"

The youth replied sullenly:

Youth: "Yes."

WPC: "Turn your pockets out."

While he was doing this, the constable asked the white man to get out of the car. Directing herself to the youth again:

WPC: "Get into the car."

The youth did, looking sullen. *He had been given no explanation as to what was happening.* Now the WPC took the white man a few steps away, out of earshot, to ask him if this youth was one of the culprits.

Man: "This black lad is not one of the ones who smashed the window."

They returned to the car, the WPC asked the youth:

WPC: "What were you done for before?"

Youth: "Smashing windows at college."

WPC: "Well, it's very funny that you happen to be here, isn't it?"

Unless the youth was a culprit, he would not have known what she was talking about.
Next, the officer decided to drive to the house the youth said he had visited.
There, an Asian man opened the door and the constable asked him:

WPC: "Has he just called here?" (She had taken the youth up to the doorstep.)

Man: "My brother knows him, but he hasn't been here today" (looking puzzled): "What's going on?"

Without giving an explanation, the constable walked away saying:

WPC: "Thanks very much."

Then, the officer drove the white man back to the shop, which was on another division. On arrival, there was a panda car there, with two PCs from that division. The WPC got out of the car to discuss with one of the constables (27 years old) whom she knew, the possibilities of who had caused the damage.

WPC: "I've got a wog in here who might have done it."

The youth, who was in the car, must have heard this, but did not react. In the meantime the other PC had been talking to the white man; now he said:

PC: "A witness here says it was three whites."

He then got into the car to speak to the youth.

PC: "Let me explain what's happening. A window has been smashed here, we don't think you did it now, but because you were in the area and you've been done for a similar offence before, we had to stop you. Can I just have your name for our report?"

Youth: (Still looking very sullen)

"OK."

After giving the constable his name, he was allowed to leave.

4 Criminal damage

A constable (aged 35) was on foot patrol at 7.30 pm when he was asked over the radio to deal with a report of criminal damage at a council flat. On arrival, the door was opened by a West Indian man.

PC: "Hello."

Man: "Hello."

67

PC: "Have you called the police?"

As he was going into the flat the man asked the constable in an angry tone of voice:

Man: "What time is it?"

The constable seemed puzzled.

PC: "Have you called the police?"

The man did not reply to this question.

Man: "What time is it?"

PC: "Twenty-five to seven."

Man: "I phoned you at twelve minutes past six, I've waited too long." He said this in an extremely angry manner pointing his finger at the officer.

The constable seemed surprised to find the man in such a state over the delay in police attendance, but remained calm, almost verging on uninterested *(this attitude was typical of this officer in most encounters)*. Then, completely ignoring the man's very angry and excited state, the officer said:

PC: "Show me what's happened."

The man ignored the PC's request and shouted:

Man: "If you had come when I called, you would've caught them."

PC: "We came as soon as we could" (and gave him a look as if to say "we could not have been any quicker, what do you expect?")

Man: "They fired at the window with an airgun pellet and they've broken it."

PC: "Nobody's got the right to break your window."

The man started to make a note of the PC's number.

PC: "What are you doing?"

Man: "I'm going to complain about this."

PC: "OK, I come from X police station".

In saying this, the constable was trying to appear unaffected, but one could tell that he was annoyed. Next the man repeated that he did not believe that the constable had come as soon as he could. The officer did not like this.

PC: "So you're calling me a liar."

This was said in a raised voice. The man ignored the statement. The constable then pulled himself together and tried to be polite.

PC: "If you get in touch with the council, they'll repair the window for you."

Man: "Come and see the neighbours."

They both went downstairs, but as they were approaching the neighbour's flat, the PC walked straight past the man into the garden without saying anything. *Presumably he was going to examine the surroundings to try to establish from where the shot had been fired. It seemed as if the constable felt that the man did not deserve an explanation, or may be the constable thought that the man would not listen to him, as he was still complaining non-stop.* The constable came back soon and knocked on the neighbour's door. He asked:

PC: "What did you hear?"

Neighbour: "We heard the noise of a gun."

The man now told them how long he had waited for the police to come. Hearing this the officer said quietly:

PC: "I'm not stopping here to listen to this" and left. He had already obtained enough details for his report, so he did not feel obliged to stay.

Back in the police station, he told another constable about the incident; he made fun of the man and made it evident he did not like West Indians. He said:

"I'm going to find his phone number and give him a few nuisance phone calls."

5 Burglary

A PC (aged 32) was on mobile patrol. At 10.15 pm he was asked to deal with a burglary. On arrival, a West Indian woman opened the door. She was in a highly excited state and said angrily:

Woman: "What took you so long? It's a good job it wasn't a murder!"

PC: (calmly) "The reason we were so long my dear, was because we were at another job when we got this call."

The woman's daughter was now standing next to her, listening attentively to what the constable had to say.

Woman: "We were at a party next door, and when we came home we found the house had been burgled. They've done the meter too. So this is what they do to you when you first move in, they ask you round to a party and they come into your home when you're not there. It must be somebody from the party, they knew we weren't in."

This was said in an irate way but the constable ignored her speculations.

PC: "I'll put the meter up here, and don't touch it, the fingerprint man will come tomorrow. I'll just have your name."

With this the woman walked out of the kitchen saying:

Woman: "It must've been someone from the party."

The constable remained in the kitchen, standing where the woman had left him. He was obviously annoyed that she had walked away and shouted:

PC: "What's your name?"

Woman: (shouted) "My name is ...."

The woman was not really aware of what she had done. She had not left the constable behind intentionally, yet the constable would not move to follow her; he was making his point. He shouted another question, the woman shouted back. Now, the woman returned to the kitchen, still unaware that the constable had taken offence. She was saying:

Woman: "Whoever done it, came from in there." (She was pointing next door.)

PC: "Well, it's easy to say, but hard to prove. I'll go and have a word with them. What's their name?"

The woman told him. Next the constable went to see the woman's neighbours. A white man answered the door.

Man: "Come in, come in."

A white woman was standing in the hall and the constable asked her:

PC: "Are you X?"

She did not seem to mind being called by her first name, and said that she was X. The party was still going on in the living room and the guests looked at the PC through the door. The woman ushered the constable into the kitchen:

PC: "Has anyone left your party?"

Man & Woman: "No."

PC: "Do you feel that everyone is trustworthy?"

Man & Woman: "Yes."

Meanwhile, the music from the party had been turned off and the complainant from next door came in. She was highly emotional. Her neighbour tried to reassure her by saying:

W. Woman: "I know what it's like, we had the same three months ago."

PC: "I'll go and see the people next door to you."

The constable left without attempting to console the victim. *He did his job efficiently, but without any sympathy.*

6. Domestic dispute

A PC (aged 29) and a WPC (aged 26) were in the police station at 7 pm when the controller asked them "Can you go to a domestic, Mrs Hussein says her husband is hitting her. Don't worry it'll be over by the time you get there."

The officers took their time in responding to the call and on leaving the station, they made a joke about "Who sane?" In the car on the way to the scene the PC commented:

PC: "You have to watch these Asians. It could have gone too far and the woman could be up the wall by now". *(Thus contradicting his delayed reaction to the call.)*

On arrival, an Asian man and woman were to be seen outside a grocery shop.

PC: "Hello, what's going on?"

Woman: "It's him, he's terrible."

The man was drunk.

PC: "Let's go in the shop, it's a bit public out here."

They all went into the shop and stood at the far end of the counter, away from the door.

PC: (To woman) "Have you anywhere to stay love?"

Woman: "I've got a house not far away, but I'll stay the night at the shop with my husband."

WPC: (To woman) "You know there's a women's refuge shelter nearby if you want to stay there."

71

The man had moved down the counter and was standing at the till as if he were waiting for customers.

PC: (To man) "Can you come up here?"

Man: "This is the counter, talk here."

PC: (Assertively) "Don't play funny with me mate, come down here."

The officers next gave the woman advice about contacting a solicitor.

WPC: "Are you worried about being alone with him?"

Woman: "It's all right. I'll leave tomorrow."

Two customers entered the shop and seeing them the PC said to the man:

PC: "Go into the back room."

The man was reluctant to go at first, but the constable persuaded him by saying:

PC: "You don't want people to hear about your personal problems do you?"

In the back room the PC pointed his finger at the man and said:

PC: "Now, my wife and I have arguments, but we solve them by talking, we don't phone the police and we don't hit each other."

Man: (Pointing back at constable) "Let me just tell you something. I've been here for eight years and I know the ways. I'm not a millionaire, but I'll be going back to Pakistan with some money later on . . . "

PC: "I don't want another phone call from your wife saying you've hit her, or else I could arrest you."

Man: "She's lying. I haven't hit her."

PC: "Well, if I'm here again, I'll get a doctor to examine her and prove it. Then we could arrest you for assault. OK mate – talk to her tomorrow, not tonight, you're too drunk for that now."

On leaving the constable saw some sugar cane on the counter and asked:

PC: "What's this?"

Man: "Sugar cane, that came from twelve thousand miles away."

PC: "What do you do with it?"

The man picked up a piece and chewed it.

PC: "Great!"

WPC: "Bye now, take care of one another now."

7. Delivering news of an arrest

A WPC (aged 23) was on panda patrol at 6 pm. She was told before leaving the police station, to check whether a youth who had been arrested and was in custody at a neighbouring police station, lived at the address he had given. On arrival at the address, a 15 year old girl opened the door.

WPC: "Hello, is Mrs X home please?"

The girl shouted "Mum, Mum". Mrs X came to the front door looking worried.

WPC: "Don't worry, nobody's been hurt. I'm just delivering a message from X police station saying your son has been arrested for theft."

Woman: "What of?"

WPC: "I don't know what of."

Woman: "What time will he be out?"

WPC: "I don't know what time he'll be out, but if you phone X station, they'll be able to tell you."

Woman: "What's the number?"

WPC: "I don't know, but if you phone directory enquiries they'll tell you. As I say, don't worry too much."

Woman: "Thank you."

Though the constable was not able to provide direct answers to the woman's questions, her manner was helpful and she showed consideration, which seemed to be appreciated by the woman.

8. Motorcycle offences

A Home Beat constable (aged 30) was patrolling on foot at 2.30 pm in a small council estate. He was just walking back to the main street, having checked some garages for anything suspicious when he saw a youth mounted on a motorcycle on the pavement. As the PC approached the youth, a look of shock passed over his face.

PC: "Is this your bike?"

Youth: "Yes."

PC: "Have you got any tax for it?"

Youth: "No."

PC: "My God, it's not your lucky day is it? That will cost you £10 straight away."

After some more conversation about the motor cycle the constable said:

PC: "You're lucky I'm not going to knock you off for riding on the footpath. It's my good will day today. Take your helmet off so I can have a look at you."

Youth (Taking his helmet off): "Am I good looking?"

PC: "Have you any tax?"

Youth: "No". (In a way which made it clear that the constable was repeating himself.)

PC: "Have you ever been in trouble?"

Youth: "Loads."

PC: "Where have you come from?"

Youth: "Work."

PC: "Where do you work?"

Youth: "I can't see what my work has to do with this."

He seemed worried that the PC should find out where he worked and he became very uncooperative and aggressive.

PC: "Why are you playing silly buggers? At the moment I'm thinking of letting you off lightly. If you want to mess about I'll do you for riding on the pavement. It's up to you. You can either tell me where you've just come from or appear at court. It's up to you!"

In view of the options presented to him, the youth told the constable where he worked and said sarcastically:

Youth: "Thanks very much."

By now, two of the youth's friends had arrived on the scene. They did not speak, but they giggled. The constable ignored them. During the encounter, a woman was watching with interest out of her kitchen window. The PC had not noticed her until she banged on the window and gave a 'thumbs up' sign to the youth, who smiled back at her; she was laughing. The constable took no notice of this. He issued a form for the production of the youth's driving documents and ended by saying:

PC: "Consider yourself officially cautioned."

There was a look of complete dissatisfaction on the youth's face as the constable walked away and continued patrolling.

9. Stolen road signs

A PC (aged 23) was patrolling in a panda car at 8 pm. The previous night a sergeant was with him and as they drove past some student accommodation they had seen two police signs which read 'No Waiting' and 'Men at Work' in one of the windows. The sergeant appeared very annoyed at this and told the PC to arrest the person(s) responsible for this the following day. Acting on this the next day the PC, accompanied by another officer, drove to the student flats. On arrival, a student opened the door.

PC: "Hello Sir, we've a few enquiries to make."
Student 1: "Come in."

They all went into the kitchen where there was another male student; the constable said to the second student:

PC: "I believe there's some road signs in the flat."

Student 2: "Yes."

PC: "Where did you get them from?"

Student 2: "We found them in the bushes and thought they would look good in the flat."

PC: "Who found them?"

Student 1: "We should all take responsibility."

PC: "How many occupiers are there?"

Student 1: "Five."

This seemed to bewilder the PC and he did not know what to reply. Instead of directing himself to the students again, he said to the accompanying PC, who had remained quiet:

"What shall we do?"

PC 2 stared blankly at him and said nothing. If the students noticed that the PC was uneasy, they did not show it. They seemed too worried about the prospects of being arrested. After a few seconds' silence, which seemed like a lifetime, the constable muttered that "one student will do" and he proceeded to arrest the student who had been in the kitchen on arrival. The accompanying officer collected the signs.

PC: "We'll be about an hour at the station sorting it out."

The ride back to the police station was uneventful and silent. Back in the station the sergeant was heard saying about the student:

Sergeant: "That will stop him from joining the police force."

PC: "As a graduate entrant."

10. Burglary

A PC (aged 23) was on panda patrol alone at 6.00 pm. He was told on the radio to deal with a burglary. On arrival a woman opened the door.

PC: "Hello you've reported a burglary. Where did they break in?"

Woman: "Through the kitchen window, they put their hands through the vent and opened the window. They took £15."

The constable asked to be shown to the kitchen, where he examined the window. Then they went to the lounge, where they met the woman's husband. The PC began to ask details for his crime report. He then said that he would like to examine the window again, as he could not understand how the burglars had got their hands through the vents.

They all went back to the kitchen where the victims explained to the constable a second time how the burglars had entered. The officer was puzzled and to cover up his embarrassment, he began to speak to the complainants as if they were rather simple. They went back into the lounge where he continued taking details for the report.

PC: "Do you mind if I sit down?"

He sat down and asked formal questions in a 'dry' manner adhering strictly to the information he needed for his report, and not chatting in between questions.

Sometimes, he did not seem to properly hear the replies given to him by the man and he showed impatience.

As the PC was finishing his crime report, there was a long embarrassing silence. The man looked perplexed, as the officer sat writing. All of a sudden, the constable jumped up and went into the kitchen alone, without giving an explanation. When he came back to the lounge he said:

PC: "I went to check for fingerprints, we don't need the fingerprint men."

Man: "Will I get my £15 back?"

PC: "Where did you get it from?"

Man: "From the social security."

PC: "You may, it's possible; go to the place where you sign on."

The constable then left the scene, without making enquiries with the neighbours. He told the observer "I see attending burglaries as collecting information to pass on to the CID and nothing else. Fifty per cent of burglaries are usually done by the complainants."

11. Racial harassment/assault

A PC (aged 31) was patrolling with another PC in a panda car at 1 am. Whilst searching for an abandoned vehicle, they received a message that 2 girls had been assaulted and that they were waiting in the phone box for the police to arrive. They abandoned the search and attended to this call immediately.

On arrival at the phone box, there was no sign of the girls. They then asked the controller if an address had been given; it had. As the constable got out of the car at the address, a man (apparently a neighbour) said to him:

Man 1: "It's all happening next door!"

Two drunken girls were standing in the garden and a man standing on the door step. They were arguing. As the PC arrived on the scene one of the girls shouted:

Girl: "He pushed me and banged my head."

Man 2: "They've been throwing bricks at my window, I asked them to leave and they wouldn't, so I pushed them out of the garden."

The girls, who were very drunk, continued shouting abuse at the man. The officer asked the girls where they lived and then he told them to go home.

PC: "I'll come round and see you in a while."

The girls did not want to go and they argued about this with the constable for some time. He remained calm and insisted that they should leave. Eventually, they did. Now the PC went into the man's house.

Man 2: "They were throwing bricks and shouting abuse about my wife because she is black."

PC: "It's all something out of nothing."

Man 2: "That's right."

The constable left, as he walked towards the car another officer arrived. He told him what had happened and they both went to see the girls. On arrival the door was opened by one of the girls' grandmother. She said:

Grandmother: "Come in."

Both constables went into the lounge. The 2 girls involved in the disturbance were there, accompanied by another young girl.

PC: "Would you like to tell me what happened?"

Girl 1: "I told you once."

This was said in an extremely cheeky way, so the constable pretended to leave the room. Seeing this, she said:

Girl 1: "OK, I'll tell you."

They swore frequently in the process of telling their account and girl 1 was making faces at the officer every time he said something she did not like. But he ignored her. Every so often, the grandmother interrupted to ask the girls not to swear so much.

They told the officer that they had been with 2 other girls and that it was these girls and not them who had thrown the bricks and shouted the abuse at the man. When they had seen the man coming out of the house, the other girls had run off and the man had picked on them, had pushed them out of his garden, banged their heads and thumped them. They insisted that they wanted to make a complaint against the man. It seemed obvious that no other girls had been involved in the disturbance and that they were lying.

PC: "So you want to make a complaint and make a statement to the effect that you don't know these girls responsible, you'll have to go to your doctor you know? It'll be your word against his ..."

The girls did not like the sound of this; girl 1 made faces at him and the other girl said:

Girl 2: "Do you know what I think of the police force? It's a load of crap!"

PC: "You're entitled to your own opinions."

He said this in a civil manner and there was not a trace of sarcasm in his voice.

In spite of their comments and actions, the girls finally decided to forget the matter. The constable had made the idea of taking the man to court sound very difficult and in doing so, he 'persuaded' the girls to drop any action. After the incident, the PC said to the observer:

PC: "It's rubbish like that I can't stand."

Throughout the encounter the constable had ignored the complete lack of deference shown to him by the girls and continued to talk to them in a civil and serious way. This tactic paid off towards the end, for the girls calmed down slightly and were a bit less cheeky.

By way of contrast, it was interesting to observe the accompanying officer's attitude. He took offence at the girls' manners and was inclined to argue with them, this encouraged even more cheekiness and abuse.

12. Vehicle stop

A PC (aged 27) was patrolling with another in a car at 12.30 am when he saw a van turning right at a 'no right turn' junction. He followed the vehicle, overtook it, put on the blue light and indicated for it to stop. A twenty year old West Indian man got out of the vehicle.

PC: "What's your number plate mate?"

The man told him correctly.

PC: "Did you see the signs saying you can't turn right here?"

Man: "No, I haven't lived here very long."

PC: "Now, I can smell you have been drinking and I would like to take a sample of your breath."

Man: "OK."

The man got into the back of the police car with the officer, while the other constable remained on the pavement with the young man's girlfriend, who had by now come out of the van. The man tried to blow into the machine, but was not successful.

Man: "I'm sorry, I've got asthma." He stopped blowing and said indignantly "I'm sorry, what have you stopped me for?"

PC: "We told you."

The man had not yet managed to blow properly.

PC: "You have refused the breath test, we are arresting you for failure to provide a sample of your breath."

Man: (Complaining) "I'll do it again."

PC: "It's too late, you didn't blow hard enough."

Man: (Angrily) "I did."

PC: "You'll have another bash at the station."

Man: "Can I arrange something for my girlfriend as it's very cold?"

PC: "She can come in the car and wait at the station."

Man: (Aggressively) "I want money out of my coat so she can get a taxi, can you get it?" Now the man kept winding down the window and talking to his girlfriend, the officer kept leaning over him and winding it up again.

PC: "Shut up."

Man: (Indignantly) "Get my coat."

The tension between them was escalating, the man wound down the window again. Suddenly, his girlfriend put her hand through the window and made as if to strike the officer. The constable wound the window up and trapped her hand in the process. The man started to panic. He was scared that his girlfriend would have her arm hurt and he shouted at the officer. There was a brief scuffle and the other officer now arrested the girl and went to look for the man's coat, which he searched. Thus, both were arrested and taken to the police station.

The man's request, to have his coat brought to him, so that he could give his girlfriend some money, was reasonable, yet it was made without a suitable level of deference and this is probably why it was denied. This denial led to an aggressive incident, which might not have taken place if the officer had complied with the man's request.

13. Vehicle stop

A male probationer (aged 20) was walking along a main road at 9.30 pm when he noticed that a transit van was blocking the road. He signalled to the driver to pull up. This he did. He was a white man, aged about 40.

PC: "Did you know that your right side front light is not working? Could you please step out of the vehicle."

As the driver proceeded to do so he said:

Driver: "I'm sure that it was working."

Then, both went to the front of the van to examine the light.

Driver: "It's a bit dim, but it's working."

The constable paid no attention to this comment.

PC: "Is this your vehicle?"

Driver: "I borrowed it from a friend."

The constable asked the man for the name and address of the vehicle's owner and proceeded to ask for a computer check on the van.

Driver: "The light is working you know."

He was now opening the bonnet to see what the problem was, and pointed out to the constable how the light fitting had fallen out of its socket. This the constable did not think relevant.

PC: "It doesn't matter that the light itself is actually functioning, the point is that you can't see it. Do you check your lights every time you drive off somewhere?"

To this, there was no reply. But the officer had delivered the question in a way which indicated he expected no answer. It was now raining and the officer suggested they stood under the bus shelter while he completed his forms.

PC: "What's your name and address?"

The man told him.

PC: "Can I see your driving licence and insurance papers?"

These, the driver did not have with him, so the officer completed the form requesting him to produce them. By now, the driver had become slightly restless. He lit a cigarette and was fidgeting. *This might not have happened if the officer had made some trivial conversation whilst competing the form and had taken the trouble to look at the driver instead of concentrating solely on the form.*

After the PC gave the driver his ticket, he began to inspect the vehicle more generally. While doing so, he barely spoke to the driver, who by now was clearly agitated. Looking closely into the back of the transit van, the constable asked the man what his occupation was.

Driver: "A market trader."

At this point the controller told the PC over the radio who the vehicle belonged to. This fitted with what the driver had stated. The driver was now left to proceed on his way with a final reminder to get his light fixed. After the incident was over, the officer told the observer:

PC: "A market trader's vehicle is bound to have something wrong with it."

14. Burglary

A male probationer (aged 19) was patrolling on foot at about 3 pm in a council estate, considered by the local police to be the most problematic in the area. Few people were to be seen, and for this reason, the observer particularly noticed a West Indian man (early 20s) dressed in overalls, as he walked past the constable. It seemed as if the man wanted to say something to the PC, but after some hesitation decided not to. The constable did not make any remarks to the observer about his presence. Thus, without acknowledging each other both continued to walk, the man in the same direction and the constable towards the right, in order to cover a different section of the estate.

After a minute or two had gone by, the same young man approached the PC. He was gasping for breath, for he had been running to catch up with the constable:

WIM: "My flat's been broken into, I think it must have been the neighbour because there's no other way in from the back, unless you come in through their balcony, and the front door hasn't been touched."

PC: "OK let's go and have a look at it."

The walk towards the man's block of flats took a few minutes, as it was a very large estate. Little was said on the way, the man merely reiterated the fact that he thought it was the neighbours that had committed the burglary.

Just as they were approaching the entrance to the block of flats, a smartly dressed young West Indian woman appeared. She said to the man, gasping for breath:

WIW: "I've been to the rent office and told them; the rents officer says it must be them (ie the neighbours) and that they've done that sort of thing before." To the constable: "He also says we should go down there after you've had a look."

The officer asked in whose name the flat was; she told him it was in hers. One assumed that the young man was her boyfriend. Little was said as they walked towards her flat, along what seemed like never-ending corridors. The young woman was visibly upset and said:

WIW: "I know it's them" (ie the neighbours).

They entered a well kept and furnished flat. A smart young West Indian woman was on the phone, and a little West Indian boy (two years old) came running towards the couple. It later emerged that this woman was the tenant's sister and the little boy her son, and they also lived on the estate.

The man showed the PC where the flat had been broken into: a glass door leading on to the balcony. The burglar had obviously left via the balcony, as the front door showed no signs of damage and was still locked when the tenant had returned. The constable examined the balcony; there was a sheer drop to the ground level. It was quite obvious that the burglar had entered from the adjacent balcony.

PC: "Whoever's done it, must've come into your flat from next door."

While examining the surroundings, the constable asked the man what had been taken. He replied that a video, a stereo, an amplifier, TV and twelve video tapes ... had been stolen. He also mentioned that the burglar had tried to get money out of the meter, but had been unsuccessful. The PC went into the kitchen to examine the meter.

PC: "I'd advise you to contact the gas board, so they don't accuse you of doing this."

The woman replied that her sister was actually phoning the gas board at that moment. The constable now sat down in the lounge and started questioning the tenant as to precisely what had been taken, descriptions, makes etc. The young man said to her "I must go back to work now," she was busily describing to the constable what had been stolen and ignored his remark.

WIW: "They've also gone through all my drawers and found the £50 I'd left inside a pair of socks."

PC: "Have you the serial number for the TV or the video?"

WIW: "No."

PC: "Have you any receipts? They're often listed on that?"

83

WIW: "I'll go and see."

As she went towards her bedroom, the young man said once again:

WIM: "I've got to go back to work now."

This time she acknowledged his remark and the man left the flat. The woman came back to the lounge with a pile of letters and documents. She was looking for the receipts (which hopefully listed the serial numbers).

WIW: "They've been through all my papers as well, I can tell, they're not in order." The other woman who had finished phoning, now said to her sister:

WIW 2: "It's hopeless looking through that, the police wouldn't find the things for you anyhow. If you were English they would, but you're black, so don't bother."

This, the PC ignored.

From now on, the tenant's sister who had said nothing, partly because she had been on the phone and partly because the man had been "in charge", started to take control of the situation. Every time the constable made a note of something, she spoke to her sister in dialect in an angry tone of voice. This, the constable also ignored; he continued to make a list of the stolen items. The little boy was now sitting next to him, observing his every move with keen interest.

WIW: "I know it must've been them because I went and knocked on her door a short while ago and she was shaking, she wouldn't let me in, she said she was busy. She was really shaking, you don't shake if you've got nothing to hide and I know her well enough to know she was hiding something."

The constable asked her if she knew the neighbour quite well. She replied that she was on speaking terms with her and had invited her into the flat not long ago. On hearing this, her sister started to tell her off:

WIW 2: "You're silly, you go around inviting the first person you meet into your house. You think all whites are good people, that's not true, there are as many bad whites as black ones. She's English, leave them at their own place. Besides, her boyfriend only came out after Christmas. Give her a good beating, if she was black, the whites would."

Every few minutes, the sister continued along these lines:

"Stop inviting people to your place; there are wicked whites as well as blacks. I'm going about my business now, because you're too stupid, you upset me."

All of a sudden there was screaming and the sound of running down the corridor. The immediate reaction of the two women was to run out of the flat to find out what had happened. The PC did likewise. (On noticing that in the excitement, the two year old had been left alone, the observer thought it appropriate to stay behind to look after him.) The front door of the flat had been left open and one could hear a woman screaming in a hysterical manner.

WW: "They were in there, they tore her blouse and she's run after them."

The observer remained by the front door hoping to see the constable and the young women returning. After a few seconds, a young white woman with a baby in her arms, came towards the observer. She said:

WW: "Those boys were after her and now she's run after them."

The observer gathered that this woman was the one who had been screaming and that she was a friend of the West Indian's next door neighbour. Next, the constable, the two West Indian women and a white girl, with a torn blouse and in a state of shock, came walking along the corridor. They went into the flat next door.

The mother of the child that had been left with the observer, returned to see if her son was all right. She took him next door and the observer followed. This flat was a complete contrast with that left behind; though identical in size, it was badly kept and furnished. In a very untidy bedroom, the constable was sitting on a bed next to the young white woman, who had a little girl sitting on her lap. Her blouse was slightly torn and showed her shoulder and part of one arm; she was in a terrible state of shock, crying and shaking all the time. The PC had his arm around her and was trying to calm her down and comfort her. On the floor were a video and hi-fi equipment. These were presumably the stolen items, as the West Indian women proceeded to take them back to their flat. The constable said to them:

PC: "I had the power to come in here you know, sorry you're having to do it this way."

The West Indian tenant then said to the white woman "Sorry you had to go through this." She was referring to the incident which had just occurred. The West Indians left.

WW2: "It's not my boyfriend, it's not my boyfriend."

PC: "OK, calm down."

WW2: "But they're going to come in."

PC: "I'll square everything up with them next door. I believe someone's making you a nice cup of tea now."

Next the constable went to the West Indians' flat and asked them if they had collected all their things; they said they had everything except for some remote controls. So, he went back to the neighbour's bedroom (she was now drinking her tea in the kitchen) and searched for the remote controls. He found one of them under the bed. This he returned and said he would be back with the other one soon. Once again he returned to the flat where the stolen goods had been found and asked WW2 where the other remote control was; she said that she did not know. He looked under the bed again and found it.

On returning the second remote control to the West Indian women he said:

PC: "You've got everything now, right?"

WIW: "Yes, except for the money."

PC: "I'll be back shortly."

The constable now went to question WW2. She was not crying any more and he asked her what her boyfriend did for a living. She told him that he was working on a building site. Then he asked her for more information about the youths that had according to her "been hiding in the cupboard" when she had come back to her flat from her friend's flat. She said that two were black and one was white, about seventeen years old. He asked her if she knew them; she said that she was sure that she knew the white boy and that he lived on the estate. Then the constable asked her when she had first seen the stolen goods; she said that she had not noticed them until she had entered the flat with him (ie the PC). (*Her evidence was doubtful because she had also been asked at what time she had returned to the flat after leaving her friend's flat and it was a while ago, at least long enough to have noticed the stolen goods.*) The woman started crying again and saying that she promised it had not been her boyfriend. The constable left her and returned to the West Indians' flat.

PC: "I really don't know how they broke into your flat without breaking into hers."

Both WIW: "There you are, we told you, it was them!"

PC: "I'm not supposed to say this, but rather than leading you down the garden path, I will. You probably won't get your money back. You see, they wouldn't have left that in the room. You can't put a video in your pocket, but you can easily put some notes in it and walk away and if you haven't got the serial numbers for the notes, no one can prove it's your money."

WIW accepted the fact with resignation.

PC: "It's a council flat, so they'll pay for the door that was damaged and you've got all your other things back, which you must be pleased about. Are you insured?"

WIW: "No."

PC: "Do you want to prosecute? It's up to you."

She looked doubtful. Her sister intervened:

WIW 2: "There's no point in a black person going to court. She's got two children starving, (ie next door neighbour) she needs it more than you, forget it."

PC: "Well, it's up to you."

WIW 2: "Your name is clean, hers is dirty. If we were whites that had been burgled, they would have taken more notice of us. Look at him just now, sitting on her bed with his arms around her. Why? Because she's white."

The PC defended himself by saying that he was not a racist, that he treated everyone the same and that he had his arms around the girl, because she was in a state of shock.

WIW 2: "My sister was upset too, you didn't put your arms round her."

PC: "I can assure you I'm not a racist."

WIW 2: "Well, maybe you're different to the others; you're still young and haven't been influenced, but never in a million years can I believe that the police treat us the same as whites. I may not look it, but I'm thirty five. I don't need your help, we've survived long enough without it. I don't need no one, I know more than all you lot put together. You could have got the address of where her boyfriend is working and gone there."

PC: "She told me that he works at X building site, and I know they're doing a lot of construction work there ... I know that some policemen are pigs, but it hurts me that you think I'm a racist."

WIW 2: "Well OK, maybe you as an individual are not a racist, but lots of other policemen are. I'm sorry for what I said, but I still think that generally speaking police are racists. I hope my son will become a policeman when he grows up, or better still, a lawyer."

The argument was over. The conversation was once again about the burglary. WIW 1 said that she considered herself lucky, for she had not got any insurance, but that after what had happened, she would most certainly take out an insurance policy. Finally, she said she would not prosecute.

Just as the constable was ready to leave, he was told over the radio to deal with a burglary at the address where he now was. The women heard this and laughed. (*The police had been notified about the burglary over the phone just before the*

87

constable's arrival, the fact that he had arrived at the scene so quickly, was because he happened to be patrolling the estate at the time and the tenant's boyfriend had informed him.)

The constable said goodbye and went next door for the final time. On seeing the constable, the white woman said again:

WW2: "It's not my boyfriend ..."

PC: "They won't take your boyfriend to court. Now, stay out of each other's way. Don't tell your boyfriend about this, or at least don't exaggerate. Sorry it had to happen." (Referring to the fact that the youths had been hiding in her flat.)

After nearly an hour, the constable left the flats. The observer asked him what he had made of the screaming and the youths tearing the white woman's blouse. He replied that he was most confused and did not know what had happened. He had just heard shouting and screaming and his reaction had been to run out of the flat and see what was going on. He said that maybe they were very good actresses and had set it all up to divert attention for he had never set eyes on the three youths. Supposedly, they had left the goods in her room, but in any case, how did they get into her flat without a key? Her boyfriend or someone else with a key must have given it to them. The officer also wondered whether maybe the West Indian tenant's boyfriend had arranged it all, as a way to find out whether the goods were in the flat. *But in saying this, the constable could not have taken into account the fact that a key was needed to get inside the flat, which certainly had not been broken into, and it was unlikely that the West Indian man would have one.*

The PC told the observer that he had taken into consideration that the black girl's flat was well furnished, so they could not have been badly off and, as they had recovered everything except the money, there was nothing much he could do unless they wanted to prosecute, which they did not. He said it had annoyed him that the eldest sister had spoken in dialect and that foreigners should not speak in another language in the presence of someone who does not understand it, if they can speak English. He continued to say that he was surprised that the little boy had seemed so friendly towards him, because his mother was so anti-police and one would think that she would have influenced him.

Finally he remarked: "I should have gone to the rents office, I forgot," but did not return to the estate.

Postscript:

Two weeks later the observer was with another constable, who was patrolling near the estate. He was in fact very near to one of the estate's entrances, when a young West Indian woman on the other side of the road shouted:

WIW: "Excuse me, Excuse me." Then she came towards the observer and said: "Do you remember me? I had a burglary ..." The observer said yes.

WIW: "Remember I said it was her, the neighbour that done it, well it was. After you left, she came to say she was sorry and that she'd try to get my £50 back, which she did ... I knew it was her, all the time I knew, so you see we were right. She told me after that she had given the keys to her flat to some boys, so they could use her balcony to get to other flats to do burglaries and then she said, 'I'm sorry, I didn't know they were going to do your flat.' Imagine! Then she said she'd speak to the boys so I could get my money back and in the end she gave me the £50."

The constable asked her if the neighbour had been arrested at the time; when he heard that she had not, he seemed surprised and in fact told the lady:

PC: "I'm surprised the lady wasn't arrested there and then! And you say all your stuff was in her flat?"

The observer explained to the constable that the 'suspect' was suffering from 'shock' at the time and maybe this had influenced the other constable's decision. Then the observer asked the 'victim' whether she knew any more about her neighbour's torn blouse, the three youths etc.

WIW: "They did it themselves of course, so it really looked like someone was after her. Then her friend screamed to attract our attention and she ran down the corridor also screaming. Then if you remember, my sister and I and the policeman ran out to see what was happening. We found no boys. Of course not, because they weren't there, they'd left some time ago, leaving the stolen things in her room. I said to her 'you're a really good actress you know, you should become an actress.'"

The constable then asked if it had not been suggested at the time that she be taken to court.

WIW: "No, we decided not to in the end, she's got little children and everything, but anyhow, the council is taking her to court, because of the damage they caused to our balcony door."

PC: "Well at court she'll be questioned about how the door got broken, so the burglary will have to come up. You can still change your mind about sending her to court. If you do contact the station."

WIW: "Well, at least I got my £50 back, I was so happy, because they weren't mine you see. I arranged an insurance the next day, but I'm still thinking about how someone went through all my belongings."

The constable was sympathetic. Then she told him that she was not happy living on the estate any more, that they had tried to get a place somewhere else, but they could not. She was frightened to walk through the estate, but luckily, she did not live too far inside it. She ended by saying that the council should improve things. The constable was once again sympathetic and agreed with her entirely and said that unfortunately everything was up to the council and as it all cost money, they would not do anything.

PC: "If ever you need us, call us."

She asked where the station was and after telling her, the constable said goodbye. Later in the canteen, the constable told another officer that he had been talking to a nice West Indian girl from the estate. However they both thought that she was the "exception rather than the rule".

15. Shoplifting/Drunk

A male probationer (aged 27) was patrolling a central shopping area on foot at 1 pm when he noticed two officers in conversation with a man. He walked up and casually enquired as to whether everything was OK. One of the officers replied that the man had just been accused of shoplifting from Woolworths and was being a bit difficult about it.

The man accused appeared to be under the influence of alcohol; he also had a severe cut on his nose and two black eyes. The wounds were not new but they still looked very sore. The officer told the observer that this man was well known to the police, and that he was a local drunk and had been beaten up recently.

The officer then spoke to the drunk:

PC: "What's up with you then, you know me don't you! Hadn't we better go down to the station and sort this thing out."

The drunk insisted that he hadn't taken anything and hadn't been into Woolworths anyway.

PC: "Well let's go down to the station and sort this thing out."

At this point the man attempted to break away from the group and one of the officers said:

PC: "Right that's it, I am going to arrest you."

The two other officers then took one side each of the man and tried to move him towards the police vehicle. He was very reluctant to be moved, and kept asking why they were taking him and saying he had done nothing wrong. The subject officer, who was not holding the man kept reassuring him, saying everything would be all right and that it would be better if they went down to the station

90

where they could sort things out. The drunk then turned his attention to the observer, and kept asking who he was. The subject officer again tried to reassure the man by saying he was not a part of this and to "go quietly". With a bit of a scuffle they finally got the man into the vehicle and the two other officers drove off with him.

This encounter was conducted in a busy shopping centre. The drunk was a 'nuisance', both to the public in the streets and the police officers. Their way to resolve the problem in this situation was to arrest the drunk and get him out of public view. In dealing with known 'characters', in this case a drunk, police may tend to take them back to the station much more quickly than with someone they are not familiar with. Dealing with members of the public that are not themselves embarrassed by an 'audience' can make an officer more eager to resolve the immediate problem and get someone out of public view.

16. Assault

A male constable (aged 32) was on foot patrol at 9 pm. He was in the process of putting a ticket on a vehicle parked on a double yellow line and obstructing the road. Three women at the bottom of the road began trying to attract his attention. At first he seemed to ignore them; they began to shout:

Women: "If he's not too busy! If he's got the bloody time! It looks like that car's more important!"

They were standing about 15 yards away on the street corner. Without looking at them the officer closed his notebook and said:

PC: "I'd better see what they want; this will have to wait."

The shouting of the women was not urgent, but they clearly wanted to speak to the officer and weren't just trying to 'wind him up'. He walked slowly toward the group. There were three of them, and they appeared to know each other. As the officer approached they made comments such as "Oh, at last", and "Now he's got nothing better to do". The officer showed no response to their comments and walked up to them in a casual manner.

PC: "What's all the fuss about?"

His manner was not unfriendly but more one of not wanting to be seen to be affected by the women's comments. After the women had finished talking about the officer's apparent disinterest, one of them started to explain why they had called him over. There seemed to be a clear understanding between the officer and the women that they were prostitutes. No explanation was made. The main participant began to explain:

Woman 1: "I got into this car, very flashy, automatic windows and seat belts."

91

The other women kept adding to her statement, seemingly to verify what she was saying.

Women 2 & 3: "Yeah really flash motor." "Silver coloured" etc.

The first woman continued with her story.

Woman 1: "I got into the car and the bloke was supposed to just drive round the corner but he didn't."

The officer did not ask her what she was doing in the car.

Woman 1: "He took me to this road, miles away, I was shit scared, then he took his clothes off. I couldn't get the seat belt off. He told me to get down on him."

The woman then shivered with horror at the thought and the other two women began to ask the officer what he was going to do about it. He then asked:

PC: "Did you get the licence number?"

The three women replied "no". They said they didn't think about it at the time. The officer then said:

PC: "Well we can't do anything unless we've got the number. Do you know this bloke?"

Woman 1: "No, but it was a really flashy silver car, ugh he was horrible, I was shit scared."

PC: "Well we can't do anything unless we've got the number plate."

The women did not seem unhappy with this comment, but throughout the conversation both parties treated each other with a certain cynicism.

PC: "If you see this car again get the number and we'll see what we can do."

He then asked the girl who had made the complaint "Are you still taking them over the road?". He pointed to a building nearby.

The woman did not reply and her two friends told her not to say anything.

Women 2 & 3: "Don't tell him anything."

He then asked the other two women where they lived.

Women 2 & 3: "We're not telling you anything."

PC: "I didn't think you would tell me."

Women 2 & 3: "Too bloody right."

This part of the conversation was held in good humour, but the women were clearly suspicious of the officer. He then changed the subject and said:

PC: "If you ladies don't go home, I bet there's a million to one chance that you'll all get picked up tonight. They've got a vice squad out and I bet you'll be in the nick tonight for prostitution."

Woman: "Loitering" corrected one of the women, "Loitering you mean."

PC: "Yeah, well there's a million to one chance, now go home."

He did not wait to see the result of his warning and walked off, he also made no further mention of the cause of the conversation, neither did the women. He quickly walked off and turned up a side street out of their view.

It is possible that the abrupt end to this encounter can be explained by the women's correction of his term "prostitution". He perhaps felt that they were more familiar with dealing with this problem than he was so best to beat a hasty retreat.

After the encounter the officer spoke briefly to the observer about it. He said that police officers (including himself) were genuinely concerned about the type of problem that the woman had raised, as every now and again prostitutes were murdered, and it was useful to know about any 'weirdoes' in the area. However, he then went on to say that most of the cases of rape that the police had to deal with were from prostitutes, and what could you expect.

17. Indecency

A male constable (aged 30) was patrolling on foot at 3 pm when a woman riding a bike passed. The officer said "hello". He did not know the woman; it was just a friendly gesture. The woman carried on cycling and then stopped about ten yards down the road. The officer at this time had stopped and was relaying a radio message to the station. The woman then tried to attract his attention. He at first did not see the woman as his back was facing her. She shouted.

Woman: "Hello! Excuse me!"

The woman was aged about 35, she was smartly dressed, and spoke with a slight American accent.

The officer turned and walked down toward the woman as she walked up toward him pushing her bicycle.

Woman: "Excuse me, I just wanted to have a quiet word with you. Is this man (the observer) a police officer?"

PC: "It's all right, he's with me."

Woman: "Well, I have something to tell you. I was cycling home last night, near the school at the bottom of this hill, you know the one."

She seemed slightly nervous and kept looking over her shoulder. At one point she stopped speaking in mid-sentence to allow some people to walk past. She was clearly concerned about privacy and the officer responded with tact. He did not speak loudly or attempt to continue conversation whilst members of the public were walking by. The woman then began to explain the reason for talking to the officer.

Woman: "I was cycling home after having delivered some leaflets; I don't often go out that late."

PC: "What time was this?"

The officer did appear to be interested in what the woman was saying. *This may have been partly due to the air of confidentiality she gave to the proceedings.* She replied that it must have been about 10 o'clock when she heard voices shouting "Excuse me, hey!" She told the officer that she did not think at the time there was anything wrong, she just thought that someone was trying to attract her attention, perhaps she had dropped something.

Woman: "Anyway I thought someone was just calling so I turned round and this boy ran down and threw something burning towards me and urinated on me. It was horrible as you can imagine."

The officer did not show any signs of embarrassment or amusement. The first question he asked was what it was that was thrown at her, was it a box of matches? The woman replied that it wasn't, she seemed unable to explain exactly what it was, and told the officer that all the kids had them, you could buy them in the shops. The officer enquired as to whether she meant "bangers". She replied, "Not exactly you know those things you can get in the shops."

PC: "What, fireworks, that type of thing?"

Woman: "Yes that's right."

There was some confusion at this point. The woman was not sure what it was exactly, and the officer was unable to define it precisely.

Woman: "I then phoned the police. I waited but they didn't turn up."

The officer took out his notebook at this point; the comment about the police not turning up was worth noting. He asked the woman what she had said to the person on the phone.

94

Woman: "I told the man that these children had thrown something at me."

PC: "So you didn't tell them about the kids urinating?"

Woman: "No, well I couldn't on the phone, could I?"

The officer seemed to accept this point.

PC: "Well that's probably why they didn't turn up. If you had said that, they'd have taken it more seriously."

The woman did not take this comment as a criticism and seemed to understand his point of view.

Woman: "The thing is that if they'd arrived they could have got them. I waited for a long time. I know where some of them live; it's that house, No 7."

PC: "Do you know which street it's on?"

Woman: "I could show you, but I can't remember the name."

The officer was taking notes at this time but then stopped to ask her some more questions.

PC: "How old were these kids?"

Woman: "They must have been about 12 I would think."

She then pointed to a child nearby and told the officer that they would have been about that height. The officer now became slightly more inquisitive. He explained afterwards that it was at this point that he began to wonder as to whether the woman was 'all there'. He was clearly puzzled as to how the offence was committed. He asked her, with some embarrassment:

PC: "If you don't mind me asking...um, well you can see, how exactly was the offence committed. I mean how exactly was it done?"

The woman then repeated the fact that she had not expected this to happen and that they had thrown some 'fire' at her.

Woman: "They all gathered round me so quickly, and then he did it, it went all over my hair and coat and scarf."

The officer then moved closer to her.

PC: "Excuse me, I'm sorry to ask this but did you see his penis?"

The woman seemed a little embarrassed by the question but answered that she had not as it was dark and she was very shocked. The officer agreed that it must have been very upsetting. He then told her that there was little they could do now but that he would get one of the policewomen to visit her. He asked her for her address and promised that they would call on her. *The woman did not seem unhappy with the encounter. The promise of a visit by a policewoman did not seem to be most important to her. She seemed more concerned with talking to the officer about it and making a point; not a criticism of the lack of response, but more that these children were a nuisance and their presence should be brought to the attention of an officer on the beat.* Her final words were:

Woman: "I felt I should point this out to you, just in case you saw them around the school."

The officer then replied "With this type of thing we only will catch them if they do it again, but I will get the policewoman to visit you."

This incident demonstrated certain aspects of encounters that involve dealing with a potentially embarrassing situation. The officer felt at one stage that the woman was mentally unstable. This could have been for two reasons: (a) He did not understand how the offence had been committed and a report that is within the understanding of the officer is more believable than one which isn't. It is not necessarily the credibility of the individual as much as the credibility of the 'story'; (b) in a situation such as this one there may be a temptation for the officer to treat the victim as an offender. Things are, perhaps, not so clear cut in the officer's mind as when, say, a victim of a theft is involved.

18. Foot stop

This incident took place at about 4 pm one afternoon. A male constable (aged 24) was driving a panda car slowly along a main road. All of a sudden, he saw two black youths aged about 14, running down a side road, towards the main road, where he was passing. The constable stopped his car just as they were approaching the main street, which was a busy shopping area, lowered the window and shouted at them.

PC: "Hoi you two, wait there!"

He got out of the car and said:

PC: "Why are you running?"

WI youths: "We were just running."

PC: "Oh yes!"

This was said sarcastically and in a way which indicated that he did not believe them. Next, he asked one of the youths to lift his arms up, and he proceeded to frisk him. What the constable expected to find was not clear, but he found nothing. Before he had the chance to frisk the other youth, the youths said:

WI youths: "We were running, that's all, we'd just come out of school."

PC: "Which school?"

This was also said in a way which indicated disbelief.

WI youths: "The school down there called —"

PC: "I thought that was an infants' school."

WI youths: "No, it's a secondary school."

At this point, two West Indian girls of about the same age as the boys appeared. One of them was extremely outspoken and said to the constable:

WI Girl: "They weren't doing anything, leave them alone. The headmistress is just down there, go and ask her."

PC: "I didn't say they were doing something."

WI Girl: (Who had obviously seen the constable frisking the youth): "So, what you checking him for then?"

PC: (Not in a very decisive way) "I'm just doing my job."

As he was saying this, the teenagers walked away; the constable did not say goodbye and did not apologise to them. Back in the car, it was obvious that the policeman felt uncomfortable about the scene, for he kept justifying his actions to the observer:

"In case you're wondering why I stopped them, it's because I thought to myself: 'what right have those two black guys got to be down there'?." He very quickly rephrased this:

"Well, what I mean is, what are those two doing down there, is there any reason for them to be there... They were running and I saw two black girls on the corner, not the two that came up to speak to me, giving them a significant look. Furthermore, I didn't know that school was a secondary school".

By now he was driving past the school.

"See, it's so small, it looks like an infants school, there's nothing about it being a secondary school on the board. Well, one learns something new every day."

97

Later on, the officer drove past some young children and he said: "These are the ones we can still win over. We've lost the others."

(He was of course referring to the age group he had stopped and searched.)

Postscript

A few days later, the observer visited the same school with a Home Beat Officer; it was a school for Remedial Education. On that day, this officer explained to the observer how long it took him to establish a good rapport with the children at this school and how, within minutes, his work could be destroyed by 'relief officers' patrolling the area, who shouted and were abrupt towards the children and had no idea how to treat them.

If the officer's knowledge of the schools in the area had been better, he may not have been so surprised to see some boys running in that road, at that time of day; nor would he have been so sceptical when they told him they had just come out of school. Most likely, the incident would have never taken place. In any case, the PC did not take into account the boy's feelings, when frisking him in a busy street.

19. Dispute at shop

A male constable (aged 22) was patrolling alone in a panda car. At about 7 pm the constable was told over the radio to go to a disturbance at a shop. On his way there, he was told to collect a missing child from an address instead. Once he had finished with this call, the constable asked over the radio if anyone else had dealt with the disturbance at the shop. He was told not. Before arriving at the shop he told the observer: "This disturbance is a few hours old and I have a feeling it may be a shoplifter."

The 'victim' was a middle aged Pakistani shopkeeper. Next to him were two women dressed in saris.

PC: "Sorry we're so late."

Shopkeeper: "The man at number two broke my shop window some time ago and agreed to pay me £5 every week (he showed the PC a piece of paper); my insurance company doesn't pay for it. Tonight he brought his boss along with him, who says to me 'you must claim it from the insurance officer, not from him'. So he wants to claim back his money, because he says I've got it from the insurance . . . "

The constable interrupted him:

PC (In a slightly raised tone of voice): "Can you listen to me! Go to your solicitor; it's not a police matter now as originally reported, because the guy isn't here causing a disturbance, you must sort it out in court."

Shopkeeper: "Can I call him?" (ie the man at number 2). Now the youngest of the two women (presumably his daughter) intervened, and said to the PC:

Daughter: "He was really shouting, we thought he'd punch him."

PC: "I appreciate it, sorry I'm so late, but go to your solicitor and then, if there are further problems, phone the police station. If he comes in shouting call us."

Shopkeeper: "But he's waiting for you at his place, so you better go and see him, otherwise he might come and shout that 'you're not calling the police.'"

PC: "OK, we'll go and see him, but please keep quiet if he shouts and swears."

The shopkeeper led the constable over the road to number two. A white man of about 19 opened the door.

PC: "Good evening, what's the problem?"

WM: "I found out that he'd got the money from the insurance."

PC: In a stern voice: "But why did you smash the window in the first place?"

WW: "You know, it was at one of those moments when he was hot headed."

WM: "That's right, when I was hot headed."

PC: "But you gave this man a written piece of paper . . . whether this man is claiming or not is none of your business. What are you worried about? Is £15 (the remainder of the payment) going to make a difference now you've been paying so long?"

WM: "But by law, is it legal if he's claiming off his insurance?"

PC: "But do we know he is?"

WM: "Yes."

PC: "Who from?"

WM: "The insurance officer."

PC: "And what right has he got to give you the information?"

WW: "His guv told him to get his policy number which any citizen can do . . . "

PC: "Yes, but what right has he . . . ? You're wasting my time you know."

As the man realised he could not win, he became less self confident and more apologetic.

WM: "Yes, sorry for wasting your time. It was the guv that had done the talking."

The PC told the young man he wanted to hear of no more trouble. As he walked across the road with the shopkeeper he said to him.

PC: "I think that's the best thing we can do."

The shopkeeper seemed satisfied and thanked the constable. In the car the constable told the observer that he had come across 'the yob' before and that he knew him as a trouble maker.

It is interesting to note how the shopkeeper and his daughter tried to persuade the constable to take some action, in spite of the man's absence from the shop. After some persuasion the constable agreed. On seeing who the 'offender' was, he was in total support of the shopkeeper. If he had not known the young man as a trouble maker, maybe he would have advised both parties to see their solicitors. Instead, he reprimanded the young man, and in doing so satisfied the shopkeeper's wishes. This was quite a change from the constable's original reactions: i.e. "not a police matter", no involvement, "see your solicitor" etc.

20. Vehicle stop

A male constable (aged 25) was patrolling alone in a panda car at 8 pm when he saw a vehicle driving in the wrong direction along a one-way street. He indicated to the driver that he should stop, which he did. The driver got out of his car. He was a West Indian, approximately 30 years old. The officer pointed out his mistake. As he was doing so, he noticed that the car had no valid tax; it had expired five weeks previously.

PC: "Why haven't you renewed the tax?"

Man: "I'm about to sell the van."

The man, who had not been uncooperative up till now, became slightly agitated and continued:

Man: "Why are you asking me all these questions? I'm not in the area to nick anything you know."

PC: "What's your date of birth?"

The man hesitated slightly and told him. Due to this hesitation, the officer became suspicious:

100

PC: "That's not your real date of birth, I think you're trying to pull a fast one over me 'cos most people know their date of birth without even thinking."

Hearing this the driver became more agitated and insisted that he was being thoughtful. Next, the officer requested a computer check on the vehicle over his radio. Ten minutes passed before a reply was given and the longer he had to wait, the angrier the man became. He was verbally hostile to the officer, accused him of being racially discriminating and complained about the delay. For most of the time, the officer did not talk to him or acknowledge his comments. But, finally he said:

PC: "I wouldn't complain if I were you, 'cos I'm not reporting you for two offences."

The driver then told the officer that he had not been driving the wrong way down a one-way street in the first place. The officer pointed out the road signs, but the man continued to argue. At this point, the computer check finally revealed that the vehicle was not stolen. As the officer was about to hand over to the man a form telling him to produce his driving documents at a police station he said:

PC: "Will you sign it?"

Man: "No, it's your form, not mine."

PC: "That's OK, you don't have to sign it if you don't want to."

Handing him the form the officer said sarcastically:

PC: "Goodbye, it's been interesting meeting you."

This remark seemed deliberately provocative, yet the driver made no response and left. In the car the officer said: "I'm going to ticket him for not having valid road tax, especially due to the reason he gave as to why. It's just not on. If he had not been so unhelpful, I might not have been so determined to prosecute him. There is no point in replying to these coloureds' questions when they're in an agitated state, as they like to talk all the time. But if you respond they get even more uptight."

21. Foot stop

A male constable (aged 25) was patrolling alone in a panda car at about 6 pm. He saw a well-dressed black youth carrying a bag, walking down the pavement. The officer commented to the observer:

"Let's give him a look. I want to see what's in that bag."

The officer pulled up the car and as he was getting out he said to the youth:

PC: "Can I have a word?"

The suspect muttered something and it was obvious from his facial expressions that he was not happy with the officer's presence. He said:

Youth: "Why are you always stopping me? I'm sick of it."

PC: "Why, do you get stopped a lot?"

Youth: "Yes."

PC: "Why's that do you think?"

To this there was no reply.

PC: "What have you got in the bag?"

He proceeded to search it. The youth protested.

PC: "If you've got nothing to hide, you've got nothing to worry about."

The youth was visibly upset and he said:

Youth: "Why do you always use the same lines?"

PC: "It's a method of stopping people, perhaps we should add a bit of spice and do it the American way, get you to kneel on the curb and liven it up a bit? By stopping people, it's the only way we're going to catch people, and if you'd had your property stolen you'd want it recovered wouldn't you?"

The youth did not reply.

PC: "Sorry we held you up, but it's only been for a few minutes."

The youth snarled back.

Youth: "Yeah, well my time is precious to me as I'm going somewhere." Then he walked away still looking upset and aggrieved. *The officer's explanations had not alleviated the situation; the youth had probably heard them too many times. In fact some of the officer's comments probably aggravated things.*

22. Foot stop

A male constable (aged 24) was patrolling with another at about 7 pm in a car. He saw a neatly dressed West Indian youth walking along a residential street carrying two black plastic bags. These had heavy objects in them, for the youth seemed to be burdened under their weight. The officer said to the other constable:

"What's he carrying? Why don't we have a look?"

They pulled up alongside the youth and the first constable got out of the car.

PC: "Hello there, the reason we're stopping you is to have a look in your bags."

The youth made no comment nor appeared dissatisfied. The officer found two stereo speakers in the bags and he asked the youth:

PC: "Where do these come from? Who do they belong to?"

Youth: "They're a present from my father."

PC: "Why have the serial stickers been removed?"

Youth: "I don't know."

PC: "There's been a lot of burglaries in the area and this is the type of electrical stuff that's been taken."

Youth: "I must go down to the station to get my speakers marked so that they can be identified if they're stolen."

PC: "Sorry for the delay."

The encounter was over. In the car the officer remarked "He seemed OK but even if it was stolen, there's nothing we could do about it, as we couldn't identify it."

The youth's demeanour towards the officer had the effect of speeding up the constable's decision on his innocence. The officer's approach, especially the prompt explanation for why he was stopping the youth, also helped towards an early resolution.

23. Vehicle stops

The following accounts describe two vehicle stops; the offences committed were the same but dealt with by different officers. It is interesting to compare the officers' attitudes towards their respective offenders and the ways they dealt with them.

Stop 1

Two male constables were patrolling a main road in a car at about 4 pm. The driver was in his early 30's, the operator in his early 20's. A few cars ahead was a van going through a red traffic light. The driver moved up to the van, driven by the middle aged West Indian man. He shouted in order that the man could hear:

PC: "Wind your window down."

The man did so. Then in a normal tone of voice:

PC: "Go past the next set of lights and then stop, we want to have a quick word with you."

Both the van driver and the police drove on. As the van continued well past the said lights, the constable was heard saying:

PC: "Where's the arse going?"

Within seconds the van driver came to a halt, and the driver got out of the police car. The West Indian man was sitting in the van waiting for him; he was dressed in painting and decorating clothes.

PC: "Hello, step out of your vehicle please, for a second, to save me getting run over."

(The constable was standing by the van driver's door and traffic was constantly passing by them.) As the driver was coming out of the van the constable said to him:

PC: "Did you see the traffic lights changing?"

Driver: "No."

PC: "You didn't see it at all?"

The man was now also exposed to the dangers of the passing traffic, and the officer touched his arm gently and said sternly:

PC: "Come in on to the pavement or you'll get run over."

Both were now on the pavement.

PC: "Do you drive up this road a lot?"

Driver: "Yes."

PC: "Well, you should know the lights."

Driver: "Sorry, but I didn't see nothing."

PC: "Is this van yours?"

Driver: "Yes."

PC: "Have you any documents?"

Driver: "Yes, my driving licence."

PC: "Can I see it?"

Driver: "Yes."

PC: "Do you work up here?"

Driver: "Yes."

PC: "Is it a company van?"

Driver: "No, mine."

Returning driving licence and with a stern voice:

PC: "Stick that back in your pocket. Next time, be more careful."

Driver: "Sorry about that."

PC: "Keep your eyes open! Cheers."

Both went back to their respective vehicles. Back in the car the constable explained to the operator and the observer that he thought a verbal warning had been the appropriate thing.

This encounter was brief and to the point; the offender's vehicle was not examined, unlike in the next example.

Stop 2
A WPC (mid 20's) and a PC (late 30's) were patrolling a busy main road in a panda car. The male constable was driving. It was an extremely cold winter's morning and there was snow on the ground. The PC drove up to a heavy goods vehicle and indicated to the driver that he wanted him to stop. When asked the reason for this, the observer was told that the man had gone through a red light.

The lorry pulled up; a middle-aged white man came out of the lorry and walked towards the police car. He was dressed in scruffy clothes and was wearing no overcoat or jersey, his T shirt did not quite cover his large stomach. As the man approached the police car, the PC wound his window down.

PC: "I was at the junction waiting to turn, you were driving down there and I saw you went through a red light."

The constable got out of the car and walked with the man towards the lorry. As they left, the WPC said to the observer:

WPC: "He loves stopping people for traffic offences!"

Then the WPC walked towards the PC and the lorry driver. Whilst the PC was making a note of something the WPC said to the lorry driver:

WPC: "Hello, you must've been in a hurry to get somewhere!" (This was said in a nice, almost sympathetic manner.)

The driver indicated to her that he was in a hurry. The male constable proceeded to examine the lorry carefully, including the tachometer, but all was found to be in order. Then came the usual checking of documents, asking for the driver's name, address, date of birth etc. All the documents were produced and the questions answered. The man made no attempt to try to justify himself and merely spoke when he was spoken to. He looked worried and cold.

The officer said in an expressionless voice:

PC: " . . . anything you say may be used against you as evidence in court."

The man said nothing.

PC: "Don't drive so fast!"

On this note the encounter ended. Afterwards the PC said:

PC: "I'll report him for the red light. I couldn't prove the speeding, though I know he was. In Germany you can prove speeding on the tachometer, but you can't here. The tachometer gives you more information about the driver, when he started, when he stopped, what speed he was doing; it's dated and it's got his name and destination. In order to see this, I made him open it and also put it back, so if it's damaged, his firm cannot sue the police. Sometimes they put in a dummy card and have the real one underneath. This was OK. I signed it and put the police number on it. He may go to court; this will be decided by the Chief Inspector or the executive officer."

This had been a 'cold' encounter, not only due to the weather conditions, but to the constable's form filling and lack of any conversation not strictly related to the offence. Some trivial conversation in between questions and especially whilst examining the lorry, and the offer to sit inside one of the vehicles or at least the suggestion that he put another garment on, would have made the offender feel more at ease.

These two encounters were similar; middle aged offenders with similar occupations, stopped for the same offence and driving goods vehicles. Both reacted to the constables with deference, did not try to argue their way out of the situation and only spoke when questioned. Yet the outcomes were totally different. The first driver was 'let off' with a verbal warning, but the second was reported.

24. Domestic dispute

A male constable (aged 32) was patrolling alone in a panda car at about 10 pm. He was asked over the radio to investigate a disturbance at an address where apparently a woman had been heard screaming. The officer arrived quickly at the address, a small one-bedroom flat. In it he found a white man and woman of about 22 years. The male was slightly upset and seemed embarrassed by the officer's presence, the female was distressed; she was crying.

Directing himself to both parties the constable asked:

PC: "What's been happening?"

The woman replied:

Woman: "He's been threatening me and he's slapped me across the face."

To this, the male said:

Man: "She's gone hysterical and won't let me watch TV because she says the lounge is her room."

The officer then attempted to discover the background to the domestic disturbance. He made each party speak in turn and he established that the man and woman were not romantically attached, but were sharing the small one-bedroom flat in order to make their small social security incomes go further. Subsequently, they had fallen out over whose the sole bedroom was. It emerged that the situation had been aggravated by the fact that the male was a very active homosexual:

Woman: "He entertains males at all hours of the night."

On hearing this the male said to the officer:

Man: "It's all right officer, she just needs a man."

This comment seemed to infuriate the woman who started to cry softly. Seeing this, the officer separated the two parties, by directing the woman to accompany him into the bedroom. Once there he said to her:

PC: "It's really a matter between yourselves, but I think that one of you should move out, it's too small for you both."

The woman agreed and said that the man intended to move out shortly. She was now calming down and the officer reunited the two in the lounge, where he addressed them both:

PC: "You're both obviously reasonable people, I can tell that you should be able to sort this out amongst yourselves. Two flat-mates should be co-operating with one another. What's going to happen when we leave here? We don't want to keep being called back now do we?"

Hearing this, both agreed that they were embarrassed that the police had become involved and each promised that they would come to an amicable agreement and that the police would have no further cause for involvement in the matter. The officer accepted this, and left. Later in the car he said to the observer:

"He was a raving queer, I wouldn't want to share a flat with him either."

It was interesting to note the officer's attempt to examine the background factors to the dispute, rather than merely concentrating on the immediate problem. The officer's form of flattery, by calling both parties 'reasonable' seemed to assist in calming them down and in encouraging them to solve their own problems. It also had the effect of making them feel slightly guilty at the police involvement in their dispute.

25. Squatters/drugs

A male constable (aged 29) was on foot patrol alone. Soon after he left the station to patrol his beat, he pointed out a high-rise council block of flats and told the observer that, on the top floor, a vacant flat had been occupied by squatters and that he was going to visit them to "Speak with them and perhaps search for drugs".

Thus it became obvious that the officer was not just 'passing by' this particular spot, but had come with a particular purpose in mind. The constable seemed to be excited at the prospect of dealing with the occupiers.
He said:

"The squatters make a general nuisance of themselves in the council block and steal electricity fuses from other flats in order to hook up electricity supplies that have been disconnected by the council."

When asked if he could arrest the occupants for squatting he replied:

"No, due to the squatter laws, but don't ask me why not; I only wish I could."

By now he had arrived at the flat, the front door was open and he walked straight into an untidy and dirty lounge. He walked around examining any articles that caught his interest such as cigarette ends and match boxes, looking for evidence of drug use. Next, he walked into a bedroom where he came across one of the squatters; he was lying on the floor half asleep. The youth was half-dressed, unshaven, unkempt and generally dishevelled. The officer said to him:

PC: "Hello, where's X?"

Squatter: "I don't know where X is." He then muttered something inaudible.

He did not seem happy with the officer's unannounced presence, especially when the constable knelt down to pick up a piece of wire and said:

PC: "Whose is this, and what is it for?"

Squatter: "I don't know."

The officer then proceeded to look through an ashtray that was next to the squatter who became nervous and agitated and said:

Squatter: "What are you doing here? You can't come in. Where's your warrant? You've got to leave."

The officer ignored him and continued to look at the ashtray. He was smiling. Then he said:

PC: "Let's have a look at your arm?"

He picked up the squatter's arm and examined it. On it, there was distinct evidence of bruising and needlemarks. The officer then noticed an empty syringe and said:

PC: "Whose is this? Yours?"

Squatter: "I'm not saying nothing. I'm not talking to you."

The officer smiled and said:

PC: "OK don't. I'm going to have a look around the flat."

As the officer was walking about looking for evidence of drug-taking, the squatter was getting up from the floor. He followed the officer saying things such as:

Squatter: "You're shit. You're just a plod, no good for nothing."

The officer appeared to be amused by the derogatory comments.

Squatter: "You can't come in here. I'm going to tell my solicitor."

PC: "Yes I can."

Squatter: "No you can't."

PC: "You say I can't; I say I can and I am."

The officer continued to look around and suddenly located two syringes on top of a cupboard. Inside one of them was some fluid.

PC: "Whose are these?"

Squatter: "I ain't talking to you, I ain't saying nothing."

PC: "You're arrested."

Then the officer searched the young man. Next, holding him firmly by the arm he walked him to the lift and then to the police station, which was not far away.

On the walk back to the station, the squatter could be heard saying to the PC:

Squatter: "You're a pig, you're a plod...Are you pleased now? I suppose you'll get a promotion. You're only a PC and all you'll ever be. I bet you only earn £100 a week."

The officer smiled, he seemed unprovoked, he did not even reply. In the police yard, the constable said to a colleague in the suspect's presence:

PC: "Look, another druggie."

The other constable replied: "Well done."

Squatter: "I'm not a druggie."

The suspect was then taken into the station and the evidence sent away for forensic examination.

26. Domestic dispute

A male constable (aged 23) was patrolling alone in a panda car at about 8 pm. He was told over his personal radio to "go to — Road where someone requires assistance with removing a person from their flat". On arriving at the said road, the PC made a comment about the area being horrible. He had some trouble finding the precise address, so he asked a couple of young West Indian men who were working on their car. Once there, a young white woman opened the door.

PC: "Hello my love, what's the problem?"

Woman: "I want you to ask Fred to go."

PC: "Who is Fred? Your boyfriend?"

Woman: "No, my ex-boyfriend."

PC shouting so as to be heard by Fred:

PC: "Fred, can I have a quick word with you mate?"

A young West Indian man came down the stairs.

PC: "I want to hear both sides."

To the woman:

PC: "Did you let him in?"

Woman: "I asked him not to come in, but he wouldn't go. I asked him to leave."

PC: "Why did you break up?"

Woman: "I broke up last week because he's violent."

PC: "Do you rent the flat?"

Woman: "Yes, I rent it."

PC (To man): "As she rents the council property, she's got every right to ask you to leave."

PC (To woman): "Do you want him to leave?"

There was no reply to this question, just a hesitant look.

The man now asked the PC:

Fred: "Can we have a quick word?"

PC: "OK, but don't lock her in the bedroom."

This was said jokingly.

While he was waiting for the couple to finish conversing, the constable told the observer that he was trying to do things in the nicest way possible and hence, he was allowing them some privacy. After a few minutes, his patience ran out.

PC: "Hurry up for Christ's sake! Is it all right to come up?"

This was said as he was going up the stairs. There was no reply. Then knocking on the door:

111

PC: "Sorry to interrupt Fred; the best thing is to leave while I'm here, then ring her up and meet in the pub."

Fred: "Just a few more minutes!"

PC: "No, because you're wasting my time and I'm trying to sort it out the best way possible."

In view of the fact that he was being asked to leave immediately the man asked the constable:

Fred: "Can't I return then some other time, to pick up my clothes?"

The PC repeated that he could phone her and meet her somewhere. Then he said:

PC: "We're so busy, we can't waste time, is that on?"

Then to the woman:

PC: "Do you want Fred to leave?"

Woman: "Yes." (In a quiet tone of voice.)

Fred now left without causing any trouble. The girl seemed upset. The constable told her:

PC: "Neither party can be happy luv."

He then left the premises. Fred was to be seen a few yards away. The constable caught up with him and said:

PC: "Hey Fred, I'm sorry, but you know what women are like, they're the hysterical ones, I've seen it loads of times. I'd rather speak to the men. Are you OK?"

Fred: (With tears in his eyes) "She says I'm violent, I don't understand her. One minute she says she loves me, the next she doesn't."

PC: "Phone her and arrange to meet her."

Fred: "But she's not on the phone. I'm paying what she owes at the moment."

PC: "How long were you with her?"

Fred: "One year, I just don't understand her!"

By now they were out in the street and the constable said good-bye to the man. Once in the car, the constable explained to the observer how he used the comment

"You know what women are like ..." as a mechanism to keep the men happy and to make them talk in situations like this. He added that he also used the same tactics, but in reverse where women are concerned.

Though maybe the constable could have been a little more patient when the couple were discussing things, he handled the encounter quite well. First, he listened not only to the 'victim' but to the 'accused' as well. He allowed the man to discuss things over with his ex-girlfriend once more, and he did not demand that this be done in front of himself. In doing so he respected the couple's privacy and showed that he 'trusted' the man. He only asked the man to leave after asking the woman a second time; he did not act on the original radio request he had received.

Finally he went to the trouble of talking to the man, once the immediate problem was over and he had, theoretically, completed his job. The man left the flat voluntarily and in a peaceful way, and the constable's attitude helped towards the resolution.

27. Landlord-Tenant dispute

A PC (aged 42) was patrolling a quiet residential area in a panda car. At about 7 pm he heard the following message over his personal radio:

"Can you deal with another one at ...?"

(The previous call had been a disturbance.)

On arriving at the road the constable said to the driver:

"It may well be some West Indians."

He was right; a middle-aged West Indian lady opened the door.

PC: "Good evening, did you call us?"

WIW: "Not me, the gentleman ..."

(He turned out to be one of her tenants.)

She showed the constable into the front room of the house and she said:

WIW: "Sit down, I sleep here sometimes."

PC: "If he called me, it's better if I speak to him first."

The lady called for someone to come down.

A young (white) man came down the stairs saying:

113

W man: "She's the landlady and she started moaning about the rent to my wife. She's rented a room to an alcoholic; we've had enough and we've asked her to move him out. He shitted the bathroom and my wife had to clean it up."

PC: "Is it the first time you've called us?"

W man: "Yes."

The landlady, who had returned to her room after calling the young man, came out to the hall and asked them to come into the room.

WIW: "I want to speak in front of him" (ie her tenant).

The constable and tenant entered the room and the officer repeated to the landlady what he had just heard from the tenant; he asked:

PC: "Can you do something about it, because otherwise the gentleman may call us."

WIW: "I don't know about this, this gentleman I took temporary. He said he was leaving and then not."

Now she directed herself to the tenant.

WIW: "Is it right?"

W man: "Yes."

WIW (To constable):
"I don't know the other gentleman as a bad person."

(She was referring to the other tenant).

PC: "He's not saying anything about his character, but that he went to the bathroom and dirtied it."

WIW: "I don't believe it."

PC: "Why should the gentleman say it if it's not true?"

WIW: "Who cleans the mess up then?"

W man: "My wife."

114

WIW: (To constable):
"I do most of the cleaning around here — Don't believe everything this man tells you. He said he's paying no rent to black people."

The tenant tried to interrupt the landlady. She would not have it. A shouting match started.

PC: "It's no good all of us talking at once."

W man: "But the accommodation agent I went to see is black."

PC: "What's the agency like, are any contracts drawn up?"

W man: "No."

WIW: "They've come to throw me out of my own house."

PC (To tenant):
"What's the position with the rent? Are you up to date with your rent?"

W man: "No, we'll pay when he goes out."

PC: "This lady is entitled to invite whoever she wants into her house."

WIW: "Don't believe him constable."

PC: "You're both saying different things, so who do I believe? You can't say for definite it isn't true" (ie that the other tenant had dirtied the bathroom).

WIW: "Well, if he does it, it's wrong."

PC: "Can you or your husband see if these facts are true and, if so, deal with them?"

WIW: "Well, if he did, it wouldn't be sanitary."

PC: "And you wouldn't be happy?"

WIW: "No, No."

Now the tenant's wife (white) appeared.

WIW: "She moved things into my spare room without permission ..."

PC: "Just a minute, I promise I'll call you in a minute."

115

Turning to the tenant's wife —

"Did you?"

W W: "Yes, but I asked her if I could after I'd left the things there."

PC: "It seems reasonable."

The landlady once again brought up the subject that her spare room had been used without her permission.

W man: "We're going away from the point."

PC: "Just a minute dear."

WIW: "My uncle is a policeman, I'm not stupid. You think I'm stupid? I locked the door so ...couldn't take my things out ..."

PC: "The reason we called was to sort out the problem about X dirtying the bathroom ..."

The constable clearly thought that she should adhere to discussing the original complaint by the tenant. The landlady was concerned to use the opportunity of the constable's presence to explain all the grievances she had against the tenant.

WIW: "Has he got the right to push me outside?"

PC: "These people will say something and you will say something else ..."

The woman continued talking non-stop.

PC (Raising his voice) "You're not listening to me."

The constable had been trying to explain to the landlady again, why the couple wanted the other tenant to leave. The landlady was not listening, she was obsessed with the fact that she was owed rent money by temporary tenants, whilst the person they were complaining about was a permanent tenant.

PC: "They said they're not paying the rent, not because he is here, but because of what he's done."

WIW: "It's a lie."

PC: "See for yourself. You may find they're right."

WIW: "Where's X going to get the money from to get drunk every night."

PC: "You can't disbelieve it, till you see it for yourself."

WIW: "That's why I'm here."

PC: "If they're right, you owe them an apology."

WIW: "Yes I'll apologise. But why are they not wanting to pay?"

The constable told her that they did not want to pay her because the bathroom had been dirtied.

WIW: "But Tuesday night they didn't say that. What do they want me to do?"

PC: "Have a look."

WW: "Even the other tenant who doesn't see him much is against him."

PC: "Where is he?"

WW: "He works nights."

WIW: "X wouldn't do it on the floor!"

WM: "Yes he did."

WIW: "But my husband was here that night."

PC: "I don't believe it!"

WM: "Her husband was here, with her son, and saw him come in drunk and said to him 'go to the bathroom and clean yourself up.'"

PC: "So, this lady's husband and son saw it."

WIW: "But they tell me nothing."

PC: "Don't tell me that ...you work nights so may be they didn't see you that day and forgot to tell you."

WIW (Pointing at the tenant):

"He came to fight me and his wife had to tell him to leave me alone."

PC: "Why didn't you say so when I first came?"

WIW To tenant:

"Is it a lie? If I want to lock my room, I do... I'm a church woman, I'm a Presbyterian member. You can't convict X."

PC: "If you're a Christian lady, why don't you listen to this man, you haven't even let me speak — if you feel you've been assaulted, go to court."

WM: "You don't want to take me to court do you?"

This was said to the landlady in a quiet tone of voice.

WIW: "I can stand up to it myself."

To tenant:

"You've got no right to put your hand on me."

PC: "Did he pull your hand or the door? Is your hand injured?"

WIW: "No."

PC: "You can take the matter to court if you want."

WM: "You don't want to take me to court, you wouldn't do that to me."

This, once again, was said quietly.

WIW: "I don't want to go to court."

PC: "Then I won't say anything more. Has this gentleman got your assurance that you'll stay here and see what your other tenant is up to?"

WIW: "But if I'm around, X won't do it."

(Leaving the room...)

PC: "That's good, thank you for your time."

WM: "Thanks for coming and assessing it."

WIW: "He told me to get out."

PC: "Whatever you tell me it'll be different."

WIW: "I'm not speaking lies."

The conversation was now taking place in the hall. Presumably to avoid yet another argument, the constable said to the tenant:

PC: "Go back to your room."

The man left.

WIW: "I have to stay around here to protect the property; my husband has had to call the police because someone stole some materials from the garden, so I can keep an eye on X."

(She was referring to the 'alcoholic tenant'.) Regarding the complainants she said:

"They come here temporary and shouldn't cause all that trouble, but I'll put him out if I see anything."

PC: "Thank you."

After thirty minutes the encounter had come to an end; the constable left. Once in the car he said:

"A lot of people of that nation (ie West Indians) you just can't get through to them. Did you notice what she said about her being black? They always swing that one on you!"

28. Foot stop

It was a 'quiet' winter evening at about 7 pm. PC1 (aged 25) and PC2 (aged 28) were patrolling a main road in a residential area in a car. There were quite a few cars about, but few pedestrians were to be seen.

A West Indian man in his mid-twenties in neat, casual dress was walking on the pavement, in the same direction (on the nearside) as the car. On seeing him, the driver slowed down without any comment and asked the operator to wind the window down. He then stopped the car and without getting out he said to the West Indian man:

PC1: "Hello mate, can we have a quick word?"

(This was said in rather a loud voice due to the distance involved.)
The man stopped.

PC1: "Where do you live?"

The man told him.

PC1: "Oh, I know you ...I can't remember your name."

The man told him and from now on the constable called him by his first name.

PC1: "What's your surname ...?"

119

This time there was no response, but the constable did not pursue the question further and now tried a different approach.

PC1: "We're just checking to make sure that no one is where they shouldn't be. Are you being a good guy?"

(This suggested that the man had 'been in trouble' at some stage.)

W I man: "Yes, I'm always a good guy."

At this point it seemed that, thanks to the change in tactics, the policeman had managed once again to establish a fairly good rapport. But this changed quickly, due to the constable's decision to continue questioning the man.

PC1: "What's your date of birth?"

Now the man started to get really annoyed and for the first time he raised his voice.

W I man: "What's all this about? Come on, what are you stopping me for? You've got to have a reason for stopping someone!"

PC1: "Come on, you know me!"

The officer was appealing to the fact that they had met sometime in the past and hoped this would suffice to calm down the man. But it obviously did not, for the man insisted an explanation should be given to him.

PC1: "Well, there have been a few burglaries around here, so that's why we're stopping you."

The man seemed to accept the reason given and seemed reasonably satisfied. He had not submitted to the constable by answering every question and had been given a reason for the stop on demand.

PC1: "Where are you going to now then?"

W I man: "I'm going to collect my little girl."

PC1: "Oh, you've got one, how old is she?"

W I man: "Eight years old. I'm getting engaged in a few weeks you know."

(For the first time during the conversation, the man alluded to a subject the constable had not brought up.)

Both PCs: "Oh, that's nice."

A good rapport had been established, thanks to an explanation and a demonstration of interest in the man's child and fianceé. No more questions were asked, but before saying goodbye, the constable said:

PC1: "We're protecting you, that's all."

Though this remark sounded a bit patronising, the man took no offence and, after saying goodbye, continued his walk.

29. Vehicle stop

PC1 (aged 22) and PC2 (aged 24) were patrolling a main road in a car. It was about 8 pm and there was a lot of traffic.

PC1: "Shall we stop him?"

He was referring to the car in front, which had no obligatory rear lights on.

PC2: "Well, he's obviously realised and that's why he's got the fog ones on."

Due to the density of the traffic, the police car was situated behind the car for some time. Meanwhile, the operator asked over the radio for a PNC check on the car; the reply was prompt. Upon hearing the owner's name and address, the car driver remarked:

PC2: "Oh I know him, isn't he the one that was involved with firearms?"

The operator said he thought so. Remarks about the 'scum' that lived on that estate (ie where the driver came from) followed.

By now the traffic had become less dense, and it would have been possible for the police car driver to go elsewhere; instead he chose to continue behind the car. This time he was not 'stuck' behind due to traffic conditions, but was clearly following it.

A few minutes passed and the driver said:

PC2: "We'd better stop him after all that."

(ie after following him for so long.)

Shortly after the car left the main road.

PC1: "Look, he's turning left."

The police car driver followed.

A few seconds passed and the car had not yet come to a halt.

PC1: "Oh, I thought it was because he was stopping for us that he had turned."

As he was saying this the car stopped.

PC1: "Oh yes, I think he is."

A young white man in his early twenties, casually dressed, got out of the car and the constables walked towards him.

PC1: "Evening mate, do you know that you've got no rear lights?"

Man: "Yes, I know, that's why I've put my fog lights on."

PC1: "They're a bit bright, that's how we noticed you. They're a bit dazzling you know."

He then asked the man for his vehicle documents. On hearing his first name, the other constable must have realised that this was not the man involved with firearms.

PC2: "Who's Z then?"

Man: "He's me cousin, nothing to do with me ..."

The reply was so fast and precise, that it was obvious the young man knew why he had been stopped, ie not because he had no rear lights on, but because his surname was the same as that of a 'criminal'.

PC2: "...and X then?"

The man replied that X was his uncle.

PC2: "So your cousin is the son of the gun guy?"

Man: "Yes."

PC2: "Who's your mate?"
(referring to the other man sitting in the car.)

Man: "He's a bloke who works for me."

PC2: "Ever been in trouble?"

Man: "No, only stopchecks."

PC2: "Ever been arrested?"

Man: "No."

PC2: "OK, get the lights fixed as soon as possible."

Man: "Yes."

After the incident had finished, the constable said:

PC2: "He obviously knows all about it, it's something that keeps coming up ...Once you start talking to people, all sorts of things come to light. He could have been reported, but it's not necessary. The guy was OK. I knew when I saw him close up it wasn't him, because he was much shorter and younger than the gun guy."

30. Betting shop disturbance

PC1 (aged 27) and PC2 (aged 26) were patrolling in a car at 4 pm.

A radio message was received:

"Could you please attend a disturbance at ..."

After making a false start by calling at the wrong address, the constables found the 'disturbance'; it was inside a bookmaker's. There were few people in the shop; near the door two young and one elderly West Indian men were to be seen. Upon seeing the constables enter the elderly West Indian man walked towards them.

PC1: "Was it you that called?"

W I man: "Yes. I do a little bit of betting here. Today I won a bit and this man (the manager) don't pay me. So, I called the operator to call you. I've never been in trouble in my whole life and I don't wanna now, so can you sort it out. He says I owe him money, but I don't."

PC1 continued talking to the customer, while PC2 went to speak to the manager (a white man).

PC2: "What's the situation?"

Manager: "He owes me money, so I won't pay him what he won today."

PC2: "Have you proof of this?"

Manager: "Yes, see here" (showing him a piece of paper).

Now PC2, who was standing by the manager's counter, called over to the customer, who was talking to the other constable.

PC2: "Come here guv, come and have a look at this."

The constable showed the customer the bit of paper, presumably an IOU which had been signed by the customer.

W I man: "This was mine, but I paid for it; I'm not telling lies."

PC2: "We're in a difficult situation, because we have to listen to both of you."

W I man: "Yes, I understand."

PC2: "We're not suggesting you're lying — we've got a problem! Haven't we?"

PC2 now suggested that the manager paid the man the difference between what the customer supposedly owed him and what he had won. This was £3.

On hearing this, the customer said:

W I man: "That's what he wanted to give me and that's why I called the police."

PC2: "Officially, this is nothing to do with the police, there's no criminal element."

This comment was meant for both the customer and the manager. He then said to the customer:

PC2: "You think you've paid the money."

This was said in a way which could be interpreted as a question or a confirmation of what the customer had previously stated.

The man said he had paid the money and then he was interrupted by the manager. It now seemed that he had also phoned the police.

Manager: "I called you, because the last time I threw someone out, he was an old man and he got hurt, and it ended up in my going to court."

In response to the manager's mention that he might be "thrown out", the customer said sarcastically:

W I man: "But I'm not coming back!"

PC1 now advised the customer to see his solicitor. While the customer was talking to PC2 again, PC1 asked the manager:

PC1: "Do you know a name for him?"

Manager: "...I've barred him 3 times already."

This remark was ignored by the constable, who asked the manager for the customer's address.

Then, the constable asked the manager:

PC1: "Can you give this gentleman your name and address?"

The customer insisted that he was owed money and was about to bring up all the issues again, when the constable interrupted him saying:

PC2: "We've got nothing to do with all this; see your solicitor about it. Do you want to take the £3 or not?"

The man was hesitant. While he was thinking, the constable said in a loud voice:

PC2: "That's obviously the problem!"

This remark was not directed at the customer in particular, but at anyone who wished to listen.

The 2 young West Indian men who were sitting in the background, had said nothing up until this moment. Now they said in chorus:

W I men: "Yes, take the £3."

W I man: "All right officer, but I wanna know his name and address Sir."

To the manager:

"Give me your name — Give me your address."

Manager: "But I've given my address."

W I man: "But this is the bookie's address and there's no name."

PC2: "This is his business address. You've got no other, so that's why you had to give your home one."

W I man: "It's a shame really, a shame that really a black person can never get a right. I phoned you to pacify this."

PC2: "We have pacified."

Manager: "Could you see him off the premises?"

PC2: "He will certainly be seen off."

W I man: "This isn't pacifying, officer."

This was said as he left the shop voluntarily. Out in the street, the man continued to speak. He was joined by the two young men.

125

W I man: "Listen to this, I don't get his address."

PC2: "Yes you do."

W I man: "This isn't the way you deal with an honest person."

PC2: "In other countries they can order people to pay money. Not here."

W I man: "But you made me leave!"

PC1: "If it had happened in your house, we'd do the same for you."

The officer decided to appeal for 'help' to the 2 young West Indians.

PC1: "Can you explain? ...or do you agree?"

Young W I: "I understand that it's not a criminal offence and that it has to be sorted out legally."

PC1 (To young man):

"Does the manager live above the shop?"

Young WI: "No."

W I man: "He's stolen money from me before. Small things really hurt. I haven't got a criminal record, not at my age!"

PC1: "Good for you!"

W I man: "He threatened me, to do me over."

PC1: "Then you've got to see a solicitor."

Young WI: "Yes, he was saying that the old man would end up in prison over Christmas."

PC1: "Have a drink now, and go to another bookie's in future."

W I man: "I'm not a gambler really, but this one (this bookie's) is convenient. I see some honesty in you. I see you can't do nothing."

PC1's attitude was obviously much preferred by the old man. He trusted him more because he had not been involved in asking him to leave the shop and furthermore, had demonstrated some interest in the affair and had sympathised with him out in the street.

PCs 1 & 2: "Go and have a drink and go to another bookie's."

As they left in the car the following remarks were made by the constables:

"The young guys were OK; they saw 'the light' quickly. That old man may have been a bit eccentric, or nutty? But then you never know..."

31. Delivering a summons

A PC (aged 30) was on foot patrol alone at 1 pm. He told the observer that he had to call at a house to deliver a message. He approached the house and knocked on the door. There was no reply. He then saw a youth mending a car to one side of the house and asked:

PC: "Hello, who are you? Is X in?"

Youth 1: "He's in the house."

By this time another youth had come to the front door and came towards the PC. On seeing him, the officer walked towards him and said:

PC: "X you've been expecting this, it's a summons for nicking cassettes."

The look on X's face indicated that he had not been expecting this news.

Youth 2: "I don't know what my Mum's going to say, she thought it was all finished with."

The officer then explained when he had to attend court and walked off leaving a very dismayed looking youth behind him.

The PC's approach was blasé, perhaps because he assumed the youth was aware of the pending summons. He did not seem concerned about the possibility that the youth may have wanted to hear the message in private. Nevertheless the youth seemed more affected by the reason for the constable's call, than by his attitude.

Appendix II: Methodology

Introduction

There are two reasons for presenting this fairly detailed account of how the study was arranged and carried out. The first is that an appreciation of the methods, their strengths and weaknesses, is essential to a full understanding of the results. This is true of any research study, but especially true of the present one. The second reason is to enable interested parties to replicate these methods. While professional researchers may find useful ideas here, the needs of police trainers are also in mind. It is not suggested that a full replication should be undertaken; rather that the general approach and philosophy of the study could be useful. This philosophy is, quite simply, that a major part of the learning process is to look at real life, question what others do, learn from their mistakes and from their achievements, and develop and test alternative ways of doing things where these seem desirable. It is important that this process should be pursued under skilled guidance and in the company of one's colleagues.

Fieldwork

Previous observational studies of policing

Much of the development of the sociology of policing during the last two decades has been based on observational research, (eg Skolnick, 1966; Bayley and Mendelsohn, 1969; Westley, 1970; Rubinstein, 1973; Cain, 1973; Bayley, 1976; Holdaway, 1983). Such studies have contributed to both theory and methodology. A number of other — often larger scale — observational studies have been carried out by the (United States) Police Foundation and others to look at the effectiveness of particular aspects of policing. One of these was concerned with women police officers, and was particularly interesting because it was concerned with 'difficult' encounters and how they were dealt with. Studies by Bloch and Anderson (1974) and Sichel *et al.*, (1978) both involved a considerable number of hours of observation — the latter study, for example, taking 3625 hours to observe 2400 incidents — and the systematic recording of information using highly structured data recording schedules. Apart from the substantive findings — one of which was that even in New York City only a very small proportion of encounters involved any physical conflict between police and public — these studies provide valuable examples of the kind of information which can be recorded by field observers.

Pilot study

Several previous observational studies used a pre-coded schedule of some kind data recording, and those developed by Black (1968), Sichel et al (1978), Sykes and Brent (1983) and McIver and Parks (1983) were found particularly useful. The original intention was that such a device would form the basis of this study. It was recognised from the start that it is very difficult to record everything which two or more parties to an interaction do or say. But the assumption was that if enough items of information could be recorded then this would provide an adequate description of what took place in encounters.

It was realised that the method of observation was a very time consuming one, though precisely how time consuming was difficult to predict in the absence of comparable evidence from studies in this country. A crucial question was just how many contacts of any substance would be seen by an observer per hour or per shift. Even the pilot study provided no conclusive answer to this, and the actual rates experienced in the main study varied considerably. In attempting to calculate any average figure the related issue had to be addressed of just what constituted an encounter. Broadly defined, this was seen as any exchange of words, gestures or actions between a police officer and a member of the public. But this includes many very brief and fleeting contacts from which, individually, it would be difficult to record very much information or to conclude much of substance. At the same time it was felt that even such fleeting encounters had something to teach, if only at a relatively general level, so that they should not be excluded from the study. The dilemma was resolved by recording only limited items of information for the 'fleeting' encounters (defined as those where no more than three exchanges took place between the officer and the member of the public). All others were regarded as 'extended' encounters, and fuller details recorded.

The pilot observations were conducted by two observers over a period of a month during the summer of 1984 in one District of the Metropolitan Police, involving some 160 hours of observation. A variety of lessons were learned about the methodology and substance of the research, and the pre-coded schedule and procedures of the study were extensively modified in the light of these lessons. As described later on, another major contribution of the pilot was to demonstrate the full part which discussion groups could play as a source of data and of analyses of that data.

Following the pilot work two seminars were held to discuss the implications for the main study with other researchers, police officers and police trainers. These were extremely productive in indicating some of the strengths and weaknesses of the proposed methods, and in pointing to the priorities which might be followed in gearing the research to the interests of police trainers.

Recruitment of observers

Observers were specially recruited for the main fieldwork. Two male observers had worked on the pilot stage and one of these was retained. He was joined by five other people, three male and two female. All were aged 25–30, an age combining maturity of outlook and some previous research or other working experience with sufficient youthful energy to follow the fairly rigorous physical and mental demands of the work. Some potential observers were rejected on the grounds that they seemed too old and might seem a little threatening to young police officers.

Although the initial inclination was to seek observers who were as similar to each other as possible, preferably all with social science training, it was soon realised that there was much more to gain from diversity than from uniformity. The academic and employment backgrounds of the observers eventually chosen included law, market research, anthropology, sociology, English and psychology. This diversity proved to be one of the greatest strengths of the project.

There were concerns at first on the part of some senior police officers as to the acceptability of women observers to police constables. These doubts proved completely unjustified. For one of the women recruited it might have helped that she was an ex police officer, but neither experienced any particular problems in becoming accepted by the police.

In the planning stage the thought arose that police observers should be included in the study. The argument for this was that only a police officer could appreciate the reasons for some of the things that the officers under observation were doing, because he would understand the legal and procedural constraints under which that officer was working. There was also the consideration that in an emergency a police observer would be able to handle himself in a way that a civilian would not be able to; possibly he might be able to assist the officer under observation in ways not open to a civilian. While these things may be true, the detachment of a police observer would always be in some question, and his presence and its purpose could be very inhibiting to those under observation. To a degree this was a problem with civilian observers, but the critical eye of one's colleagues is probably more of a threat than that of an outsider. A tentative proposal was actually made to use a police observer in the study, but this was clearly not acceptable to some supervising officers; there was concern about accepting an officer from another force or division to, as it was seen, sit in judgement upon the local officers. The proposal was, therefore, dropped.

This did not mean losing police insights into the data, for two reasons. One was that there was an ex police officer (with eight years' experience) already on the research team. A second reason was that the intention had been formulated of inviting a police presence to most of the observer meetings to help interpret the observational material.

131

Finally, whatever the case for using police insights in the research process, it must be remembered that police constables are still human beings and much of what they do can be understood by lay persons simply as human behaviour. There are special features to it but it is not something totally unique because of this. Also, the observation was not concerned simply with what the police participants did or said in encounters, but was equally concerned with how members of the public behaved; for this it was important to have observers with a non-police perspective.

Selection of forces

The problems of police-public relations are normally seen as urban problems; if only because they contain more people, cities produce numerically more cases of conflict or ill feeling between police and members of the public and, as far as police-black relations are concerned, the problems are almost entirely urban based. It is certainly more economical to use urban sites though, even there, the rate of contact between a police officer and the public can be very low. Even in busy areas the number of contacts an officer has which amount to more than giving directions are much fewer than some might believe, though there is considerable variation.

For these reasons urban sites were selected for the study, two in London, two in Birmingham and two in Bristol. In each case observers spent five weeks at one police station and then moved to the other. One particular concern was to include some areas where a fair proportion of contacts could be expected between police and ethnic minorities, so the selection was made partly with this in mind. In doing this some of the more obvious locations were excluded on the grounds that they had already been 'overresearched' or that they were particularly sensitive areas where the police were reluctant to accept observers.

The intention was to divide observation time equally between the three forces but, because of observers' varying availability just over one third of the 238 observation sessions were in the West Midlands, just over a quarter in Avon and Somerset and 40% in the Metropolitan Police areas.

Sampling of constables

During the fieldwork period police officers from all over the country were being sent to police the picket lines in the miners' strike then current. This meant some depletion of manpower available for normal patrol duties, raising two questions for the study. First, was a 'normal' policing situation being observed? It was not within the scope of the study to make comparisons of police practice between strike and non-strike conditions, and one can only speculate as to any differences. Comparison with observations during other studies under 'normal' conditions suggested that there were no qualitative differences in police behaviour, nor was there evidence of particular tasks being ignored or favoured. Reduced manpower during the strike generally meant that preemptive policing, if anything, would suffer; public demand for police services would, however, be unlikely to change, so that the study may conceivably have included more such work than it might have done at other times.

A second question raised by the unusual manpower situation is whether it led to an unrepresentative selection of officers being observed. Officers were generally selected for picket patrol duty on a rotating basis for one or two weeks at a time. Thus, the five weeks spent by observers at each police station meant that any officer there was only away on picket duty for a maximum of two fifths of the period of observation. Assuming that no particular criteria (other than sex) were used in choosing officers for picket patrol duty one can be fairly confident that a representative selection was included in the study. The general conclusion about possible biasing effects of the miners' strike is that it did not seriously change the nature or the quality of the contacts which were observed, or the kinds of officers who were observed dealing with them.

The policing of miners' picket lines is just one reason why there is rarely what could be called a 'normal' manpower situation to be found in most police stations. Shift changes, sickness, secondments, training courses, court appearances, prisoner escorts, special assignments and other demands all take a tremendous toll on available manpower (Jones, 1980; Kinsey, 1985) so that it is really very difficult to predict from day to day, or sometimes from hour to hour, just which constables are likely to be available for patrol duties. For this reason it was difficult to achieve a very precise sample of officers. The first priority was to have a constable to observe on duty at a particular time; in practice, considerations of who he was had to take second place.

However, a list was drawn up of the likely distribution of manpower during the study period and a quota of officers for observation was established, taking account of duties, sex, age and experience, so that the quota was filled during the fieldwork period as a whole.

A total of 149 constables were observed; 131 male and 18 female, slightly overrepresenting the present proportion of women officers within the three forces as a whole. 87% were under 40, 62% were under 30, and only 3% under 21. Only 5% were probationers, but they were deliberately underrepresented because it was felt that the work done by more experienced officers would be more useful to draw upon. The average (median) length of service of those observed was 6 years.

Of these constables, 86% were currently deployed as uniformed patrol officers, 9% were designated as Home/Community/Permanent Beat officers, and 5% were probationers. No CID or other officers outside the uniformed divisions were included in the study.

Police officers point out that the nature of policing can vary significantly from one time of day to another; there are normally more people both awake and on the streets during the day than at night, some areas are busy during the evening

133

hours while others are deserted, and drink related offences and problems are most likely to occur in the evenings. Police records and research (eg Hough, 1980; Ekblom and Heal, 1982) — make it clear that the early hours of the morning produce the fewest calls for police service, and that Fridays and Saturdays tend to be the busiest days of the week for the police. The study was not concerned with any particular type of contact between police and public, and it was vital to use observer time to best effect, so that although all days and hours of the day were represented, the emphasis was put upon the later days of the week and on the hours between 2 pm and midnight. Within those hours observers arranged their schedules to take account of shift starting times and the activities of particular officers. (It was quite common, for example, that a session of observation began with one officer but was prematurely terminated because the officer had to leave street patrol to deal with a prisoner or perform other work inside the police station, and in this event, the normal procedure was for the observer to go out with another officer.) Thus, 16% of observation sessions began in the morning hours up to 10am, 32% began between then and 2pm, 20% between then and 5 pm, and 32% between 6 pm and midnight.

If the officer volunteered the information or if it was very obvious, observers made a note of any factors which could conceivably affect his or her general quality of performance on that shift, such as tiredness, illness, personal or job problems. It is of interest that in one observation session in five one or more such factors was mentioned; possibly more officers were suffering from such potential stress factors than was recorded, though no firm conclusions can be drawn as to whether these affected their performance.

Data were recorded only for individual officers, though in half the sessions of observation the officer concerned was with another for all or part of the time and it is important to note the value of team work in some situations. But where there are two officers involved in an encounter they will often move around separately and hold simultaneous conversations with different members of the public; typically this is done in disputes where the officers may take the parties into separate rooms to hear each side of the story. Clearly in such conditions the observer could not always get a complete picture of what was happening, and the study therefore concentrated upon what the individual 'subject' officers did.

A balance was needed between observation of foot patrol and car patrol officers. There was some temptation to emphasise car patrol because this seemed likely to produce a more rapid succession of encounters and, thus, more data for analysis. On the other hand, given that foot patrol officers are far more 'visible' to the public and that people tend to express a strong preference for more foot patrol, it was important also to examine the quality of this type of patrol work. In practice, the distinction between foot and car patrol can become blurred where an officer finds himself doing both even during the course of one shift. In the event, three quarters of the observed sessions took place in a vehicle for at least some of the time.

The amount of contact with the public varied considerably between sessions, but it is of interest at this point to summarise the level of contact observed. There was no public contact at all in one in 20 of the sessions. In two thirds of the sessions up to a quarter of the total time was spent in contact. In one in four sessions between a quarter and a half the total time was spent in contact. And in one session in 20 between 50% and 80% of the time was spent in contact with the public. The rest of the time was spent largely in patrol, with varying numbers of visits to police premises or doing jobs which involved no public contact at all. Four out of five sessions involved at least one visit to police premises. No data were recorded by observers during such visits, observation being confined to encounters outside police premises. Apart from any encounters with the public, one quarter of the sessions involved one task involving no public contact, and another quarter involved between two and six such tasks.

Observational methods

A perennial but important question raised about all observational research is the extent to which the presence of an observer affects the behaviour of those under observation. Most observers of the police have addressed this issue at some point, and with varying degrees of concern, but none have seriously questioned the validity of observational data as a way of recording what police officers do (eg McCall, 1975; Reiss, 1979; Softley, 1980; Steer, 1980; Smith and Gray, 1983).

One can, of course, think in terms of a continuum within observational research which goes from totally non-participative to totally participative, and a related dimension is the extent to which the observer's role is known and understood by those under observation. In the present study the observers were non-participant except in rare circumstances, and no attempt was made to conceal the presence of the observer from either police or public. No pretence was made as to what the study was about or what the observer would be doing. This was explained to officers being observed both on paper in an advance briefing note and verbally by the observer. The initial stages of the observer-officer relationship normally involved some suspicion as to what was being done, and every opportunity was taken to reassure the 'subject' officers; it was also clearly stated to superior officers that no reporting back would take place on the quality of individual officers' work. Despite any secret suspicions they retained, officers under observation seemed to accept the situation quickly and got on with the job they had to do. If they were doing it in any way differently then one must assume that this would be by doing everything rather more carefully than usual and following the correct procedure in all cases. Any problems which were observed might, therefore, have been even worse when officers were not on their 'best' behaviour. However, since officers are often responding quite rapidly to events and the behaviour of others, it seems unlikely that they can substantially monitor and modify their own behaviour at the same time so as to always show themselves in the best light.

Concern was expressed by both managers and patrol officers consulted during the course of the study that it might simply produce critical findings similar to those of Policy Studies Institute research on the Metropolitan Police (Smith and Gray, 1983). While not denying this possibility, great care was taken to emphasise the different purpose of the current study, with its focus upon the observation of the day to day experiences of uniformed patrol officers as an aid to training development. It was also stressed that the observation was concerned not simply with police behaviour but equally with that of members of the public.

A further, though probably less significant, concern was how the presence of an observer might affect members of the public with whom the observed officers came into contact. Although they were equally under observation, they were probably far less aware of this, and only very rarely was an observer's identity or purpose questioned. Their appearance with the police presumably provided enough explanation for most people; they were probably CID officers or, at any rate, had some legitimate purpose. A few did question who they were and they were told the truth. If they pressed the matter further they were given an officially headed letter from the Home Office Research and Planning Unit explaining the project and inviting them to telephone the researchers for further information. In the event, few letters were needed and nobody telephoned. Again, the prime concern of the member of the public was their dealings with the officer, so that the presence of anyone else became a secondary consideration.

If an observer stands close by those he is observing making notes in a very obvious manner as they speak and act, or even recording their words on tape, this could easily inhibit those people. Some observational studies appear to have been conducted in such a manner, though most have been more discreet. Sykes and Brent (1983) used hand-held coding devices involving the punching of codes on to electronic tape for each piece of information during the encounter, and other researchers have used unobtrusive throat microphones to dictate notes while in the field. Such electronic aids clearly have attractions but can suffer from breakdown and misuse, and there was not time in this study to develop their use to acceptable levels of accuracy and reliability.

Other ideas considered at the planning stage were the use of sound or video recording of the words and actions of police and public; this would indeed be the most reliable way to record events. But there would be technical problems of getting microphones or cameras into the right place at the right time, there would be ethical problems about recording people against their will or without their knowledge, and the danger of inhibiting people's words and actions could be much increased. For all these reasons such methods were not used in the study.

From the observer's point of view, not being able to record copious data at the time of an encounter raises problems of memory; after several hours of observation the mind can become confused without some reminders of events. The method was therefore, for observers to take with them into the field a small notebook into which they noted as many significant facts as conditions allowed during — or preferably just after — each observed encounter: times, number and type of people involved, nature of the problem, locations etc. At the end of each session of observation observers then transcribed this information and expanded it in two ways. First, they completed a 'General shift information form' for the session as a whole and a 'Contact form' for each encounter observed during it. The contact form included as much information about the encounter as could reasonably be reduced to pre-coded form, extending to nine pages.

It was clear from an early stage in the piloting of these documents that they alone would not adequately capture the nature and subtleties of many encounters, especially the more extended or complex ones. It was, therefore, decided to supplement the forms with a second method of data recording: a narrative prose account of what took place. Again, the observer completed this after the event, and included extracts from the dialogue which illustrated a particular mood or turning point in the encounter, descriptions of individual behaviour, circumstances, context, or anything else judged to be relevant to an understanding of the dynamics of that encounter.

Analysis and Interpretation

Classifying problems

In looking at problems in a way useful for trainers there are a number of dimensions within which they might be classified and ordered. Two were chosen, though these also draw in further dimensions. The first of these reflects the different types of incidents encountered by the officers in the study. These can be grouped with varying degrees of specificity or generality. At the specific level, for example, one could consider what happens in traffic stops, in domestic disturbance calls, or in calls to burglary victims. More generally, one might group these into police-initiated or public-initiated contacts, into 'adversarial' as against 'consumer' contacts (see Southgate and Ekblom, 1984), or into broad classes of incident such as general enquiries, crime-related calls, contacts with juveniles and so on.

The second dimension to be used takes account of types of human relations problems or issues which arise during the course of the encounters; these sometimes arise in a wide range of circumstances and sometimes they are incident-specific. Thus, the main text considers problems under such headings as opening manner, emotional people, privacy, changing sides, and control and deference.

Those who have observed police-public encounters tend to agree that to understand them it is essential to think not in terms of a discrete event but in terms of a process with a number of stages, such as the three stage division proposed by Bayley and Bittner (1985) into entry, processing and resolution. Most of the problems observed did relate to one of these three stages and are discussed in this order, though it did not seem that police actions were necessarily specific to one particular stage of the encounter.

Judging police behaviour

Whatever classification system was used, the study needed to offer some kind of judgement of police handling of encounters. In doing so, the major emphasis has not been put upon legal and procedural aspects, but on human relations problems and issues. Judgements are made not in legalistic terms but with a view to seeing how good relations can be maximised. Moral judgements are avoided as much as possible. Behaviour was judged first in its immediate setting, though with reference to surrounding circumstances: historical, legal, social etc, as far as it was possible to be aware of these. Nevertheless, at various points the question was raised of criteria for judging 'good' and 'bad' police handling of situations. There seemed to be several ways of doing this.

First, one might look at encounters primarily from a police point of view. But this raises the problem of which police point of view this is to be: the officer on the beat, the supervisor or the higher management? Each of these is likely to have rather different concerns and priorities which could lead to different ways of handling a particular situation (Holdaway, 1977).

A second option is to judge events by purely legal standards. This might reasonably be assumed to provide an objective and widely accepted criterion. In some cases this may be appropriate and, where there is a legally unambiguous situation to deal with, there might be little problem. Unfortunately, though, as any police officer or observer of police officers can confirm, the legal definitions and choices involved in everyday policing are frequently rather obscure and, in many cases can also be inapplicable or irrelevant.

A third option is to judge police behaviour by taking account of the views of the people they come into contact with. The difficulty here is that, unless the encounters to which respondents refer can somehow be known and independently measured, then it is very difficult to establish clear links between experiences and perceptions. An alternative is to question those known from police records to have been in contact with the police on particular occasions. This was done in Ekblom and Heal's (1982) study of public calls to the police, which conducted interviews with members of the public who were recorded as having telephoned the police for some assistance.

The conditions under which the present study was conducted, however, made it very difficult to combine observation with interviewing members of the public without damaging the observer's relationship with police officers and creating logistical problems. Also, immediately after an encounter might not be the best time to question people, because their views about the officer could well change upon later reflection or in the light of some subsequent event. (And, without knowledge of when such change occurred, one could not specify what interval should elapse before the interview. There would then be a problem of locating the person for interview; in many cases the officer would not normally have asked for and recorded the person's name, address and/or telephone number and some people might question his reasons for doing so or even give false information.

Even once this information was obtained there would be problems in locating the person at that address or telephone number. This would consume considerable resources and it was not felt justifiable to divert such effort from the main activity of observing police-public interaction.) Every attempt was made by observers to record all signs of public reaction to the police officer; demeanour, tone of voice, apparent emotional state and any overt expressions of satisfaction or dissatisfaction with the police were routinely recorded.

These indicators contribute something towards a judgement of the quality of police actions but they are not enough. The best approximation to a criterion for judgement was felt to be that of the 'reasonable man', a familiar concept which combines the common sense public view with a recognised legal standard. It is not foolproof but it provided a more objective view than simply the personal feelings of the observer. Thus, in judging any piece of behaviour, what the observers had to ask themselves was how a 'reasonable man or woman' would have seen it and reacted to it.

Observer meetings

Pilot work confirmed that a pre-coded schedule alone would not give a sufficiently full picture of the dynamics of interpersonal encounters, and the need for supplementary prose accounts was recognised from an early stage. What was not originally fully recognised was the part which systematic discussion could play as a method of data processing and interpretation. During the pilot stage of the research there were frequent meetings with the two observers involved. The intended purpose of these meetings was to review how the data recording schedule was working, with a view to progressively amending it as the pilot work progressed. But it became obvious that the very act of discussing together the content of the observations was also itself a creative process in which data were being ordered and analysed. Although neither of the two observers had previous experience of police research or the literature on policing, they very quickly began to present a cogent analysis of many of the main concepts which are by now familar to researchers in this field. As in the main study itself, not all of these concepts were directly relevant to police-public interaction or had training implications, but many of them were, and it was, therefore, decided to use meetings with observers as a major part of the data analysis procedure.

There would thus be three complementary forms of evidence: the coded schedules, the prose accounts, and the thoughts, ideas and interpretations offered in discussion. They would all be based on the same observations by the same observers but they would be processed in different ways. The particular contribution of the meetings would be to ensure that each piece of data under discussion was exposed to as many alternative interpretations as there were people at the meeting. This can be seen as a modified form of 'triangulation', where the same phenomena are studied by different persons or different forms of data gathering (Denzin, 1970). Although individual observers were responsible in the short term for deciding what to record from the events they witnessed, the perceptions they offered would be open to challenge and amendment by others who had witnessed similar things. The manner of proceeding was for observers to put forward their observations in the form of hypotheses about behaviour in encounters. These were then discussed, modified or added to, so that by the end of fieldwork a list of several hundred had been assembled. They have been grouped and presented as a series of problems for consideration by practitioners; the intention is not to try to 'prove' or 'disprove' any particular assertions, but to suggest ideas.

Meetings were held at weekly or fortnightly intervals on ten occasions during the fieldwork period. In addition to those directing the study, they included the six observers (one of whom had also worked on the pilot study), the other pilot observer, and a series of invited guests. With one exception these guests were police officers; one had operational responsibilities at the time, but most were involved in either training, research or both. Their contributions were seen as important for two reasons. First, as a practical counterbalance to any over fanciful ideas the rest of the meeting might produce, and a source of reference on practical policing issues and points of law and procedure. Second, as representatives of the more immediate 'customers' for the research findings, namely the police training world.

The meetings worked well; the guests found them useful and interesting and felt that they were developing ideas which could contribute to training. From the observers' point of view they were important as a way of comparing ideas and experiences and as a means of maintaining a team spirit in what might otherwise be a very lonely enterprise; without such support it is easy for the lone observer to 'go native' and become overly absorbed into the social world he is studying. From a research point of view they were analytically fruitful and they also performed vital administrative and quality control functions.

The evaluative comments and recommendations in the main text are based upon what was observed, but it must be stressed that they are suggestions rather than proven remedies. In some cases there was frequent evidence of a problem, but this was not always so. The research was primarily qualitative in nature; that is to say it is set out not simply to count certain elements of human behaviour, but to observe this behaviour with a view to understanding and interpreting it.

References

Argyle, M. (1969). *Social Interaction.* London: Methuen.

Bard, M. (1970). *Training Police as Specialists in Family Crisis Intervention.* Washington DC: US Government Printing Office.

Bayley, D. (1976). *Forces of Order: police behaviour in Japan and the United States.* Berkeley: University of California Press.

Bayley, D. H. and Bittner, E. (1985). 'Learning the skills of policing.' In: Special edition of the *Journal of Law and Contemporary Social Problems.*

Bayley, D. H. and Mendelsohn, N. (1969). *Minorities and the Police: confrontation in America.* New York: Free Press.

Bittner, E. (1970). *The Function of the Police in Modern Society.* Washington DC: US Government Printing Office.

Black, D. (1968). *Police Encounters and Social Organization: an observational study.* Doctoral dissertation. University of Michigan.

Bloch, P. B. and Anderson, D. (1974). *Policewomen on Patrol.* Washington DC: Police Foundation.

Bull, R. (1985). 'Police awareness training'. *Policing,* 1, pp. 109–123.

Cain, M. (1973). *Society and the Policeman's Role.* London: Routledge and Kegan Paul.

Comrie, M. D. and Kings, E. J. (1974). 'Urban workloads'. *Police Research Bulletin* No. 23. London: Home Office.

Dix, M. C. and Layzell, A. D. (1983). *Road Users and the Police.* London: Croom Helm.

Denzin, N. K. (1970). *The Research Act.* Chicago: Aldine.

Ekblom, P. (1986). 'Community policing: obstacles and issues'. In Walker, A., Ekblom, P. and Deakin, N. *The Debate About Community.* London: Policy Studies Institute.

Ekblom, P. and Heal, K. (1982). *The Police Response to Calls from the Public.* Home Office Research and Planning Unit Paper No. 9. London: Home Office.

Field, S. and Southgate, P. (1982). *Public Disorder.* Home Office Research Study No. 72. London: HMSO.

Garratt, G. A., Baxter, J. C. and Rozelle, R. M. (1981). 'Training university police in black American non-verbal behaviour'. *Journal of Social Psychology, 113, pp. 217-229.*

Goffman, E. (1971). *Relations in Public.* Harmondsworth: Penguin.

Hall, E. T. (1966). *The Hidden Dimension.* New York: Doubleday.

Holdaway, S. (1977). 'Changes in urban policing'. *British Journal of Sociology,* 28, pp. 119–137.

Holdaway, S. (1983). *Inside the British Police.* Oxford: Basil Blackwell.

Home Office (1983). *Community and Race Relations Training for the Police.* Report of the Police Training Council Working Party. London: Home Office.

Home Office (1983). *The Training of Probationary Constables.* Initial Course: Student's lesson notes. London: HMSO.

Home Office (1985). *Report of the Commissioner of Police of the Metropolis for the year 1984.* Cmnd 9541. London: HMSO.

Hough, M. (1980). *Uniformed Police Work and Management Technology.* Home Office Research Unit Paper No. 1. London: Home Office.

Jones, J. M. (1980). *Organisational Aspects of Police Behaviour.* Farnborough: Gower.

Jones, S. (1983). 'The human factor and policing'. *Home Office Research and Planning Unit Bulletin* No 16. pp. 9–12.

Kinsey, R. (1985). *Survey of Merseyside Police Officers.* Merseyside County Council.

Landis, D. and Brislin, R. W. (1983). *Handbook of Intercultural Training Vol II: Issues in Training Methodology.* New York: Pergamon.

Manning, P. (1977). *Police Work: the social organisation of policing.* London: MIT Press.

McCall, G. J. (1975). *Observing the Law: applications of field methods to the study of the criminal justice system.* Washington DC: US Government Printing Office.

McIver, J. P. and Parks, R. B. (1983). 'Evaluating police performance: identification of effective and ineffective police actions'. In: **Bennett, R. R. (ed),** *Police at Work: policy issues and analysis.* Beverley Hills: Sage.

National Institute of Justice. (1985). *Replicating an Experiment in Specific Deterrence: alternative police responses to spouse assault.* Research Solicitation. Washington DC: National Institute of Justice.

NOP. (1981). 'Public losing trust in police'. *The Observer,* 15 November.

Pate, T. *et al.* (1976). *Police Response Time: its determinants and effects.* Washington DC: Police Foundation.

Pendleton, D. *et al.* (1984). *The Consultation: an approach to learning and teaching.* Oxford: Oxford University Press.

Punch, M. (1979). 'The Secret Social Service'. In: **Holdaway, S.** *The British Police.* London: Edward Arnold.

Punch, M. and Naylor, T. (1973). 'The Police — a Social Service'. *New Society,* 24, pp. 358–361.

Reiner, R. (1978). *The Blue Coated Worker: a sociological study of police unionism.* Cambridge: Cambridge University Press.

Reiner, R. (1985). *The Politics of the Police.* London: Wheatsheaf Books.

Reiss, A. J. (1971). *The Police and the Public.* New Haven: Yale University Press.

Reiss, A. J. (1979). 'Systematic social observation in police research'. In: **Knutsson, J. Kuhlhorn, E. and Reiss, A. J.,** *Police and the Social Order.* Stockholm: National Swedish Council for Crime Prevention.

Rubinstein, J. (1973). *City Police.* New York: Farrar, Straus and Giroux.

Sherman, L. and Berk, R. (1984). *The Minneapolis Domestic Violence Experiment.* Washington DC: Police Foundation.

Sichel, J. L. *et al.* (1978).*Women on patrol; a pilot study of police performance in New York City.* Washington D.C: US Department of Justice.

Skolnick, J. (1966). *Justice Without Trial.* New York: Wiley.

Smith, D. J. and Gray, J. (1983). *Police and People in London.* London: Policy Studies Institute.

Softley, P. *et al.* (1980). *Police Interrogation: an observational study in four police stations.* Home Office Research Study No. 61. London: HMSO.

Southgate, P. (1982). *Police Probationer Training in Race Relations.* Home Office Research and Planning Unit Paper No. 8. London: Home Office.

Southgate, P. (1984). *Racism Awareness Training for the Police.* Home Office Research and Planning Unit Paper No. 29. London: Home Office.

Southgate, P. and Ekblom, P. (1984). *Contacts Between Police and Public: findings from the British Crime Survey.* Home Office Research Study No. 77. London: HMSO.

Steer, D. (1980). *Uncovering Crime: the police role.* Research Study No 7 for the Royal Commission on Criminal Procedure. London: HMSO.

Sykes, R. E. and Clark, J. P. (1975). 'A theory of deference exchange in police-citizen encounters'. *American Journal of Sociology,* 81, pp. 584–600.

Sykes, R. E. and Brent, E. E. (1983). *Policing: a social behaviourist persepctive.* New Brunswick: Rutgers University Press.

Van Maanen, J. (1984). *Inside Out: observations on control in police organisations.* Paper given at Home Office seminar, 21 March.

Westley, W. (1970). *Violence and the Police.* Cambridge, Mass.: MIT Press.

Publications

Titles already published for the Home Office

Studies in the Causes of Delinquency and the Treatment of Offenders (SCDTO)

1. Prediction methods in relation to borstal training. Hermann Mannheim and Leslie T. Wilkins, 1955 viii + 276pp. (11 340051 9).

2. *Time spent awaiting trial. Evelyn Gibson. 1960. v + 45pp. (34-368-2).

3. Delinquent generations. Leslie T. Wilkins. 1960. iv + 20pp. (11 340053 5).

4. *Murder. Evelyn Gibson and S. Klein. 1961. iv + 44pp. (11 340054 3).

5. Persistent criminals. A study of all offenders liable to preventive detention in 1956. W. H. Hammond and Edna Chayen. 1963. ix + 237pp. (34-368-5).

6. *Some statistical and other numerical techniques for classifying individuals. P. McNaughton-Smith. 1965. v + 33pp. (34-368-6).

7. Probation research: a preliminary report. Part I. General outline of research. Part II. Study of Middlesex probation area (SOMPA). Steven Folkard, Kate Lyon, Margaret M. Carver and Erica O'Leary. 1966. vi + 58pp. (11 340374 7).

8. *Probation research: national study of probation. Trends and regional comparisons in probation (England and Wales). Hugh Barr and Erica O'Leary. 1966. vii + 51pp. (34-368-8).

9. *Probation research. A survey of group work in the probation service. Hugh Barr. 1966. vii + 94pp. (34-368-9).

10. *Types of delinquency and home background. A validation study of Hewitt and Jenkins' hypothesis. Elizabeth Field. 1967. vi + 21pp. (34-368-10).

11. *Studies of female offenders No. 1 — Girls of 16–20 years sentenced to borstal or detention centre training in 1963. No. 2 — Women offenders in the Metropolitan Police District in March and April 1957. No. 3 — A description of women in prison on January 1, 1965. Nancy Goodman and Jean Price. 1967. v + 78pp. (34-368-11).

12. *The use of the Jesness Inventory on a sample of British probationers. Martin Davis. 1967 iv + 20pp. (34-368-12).

13. *The Jesness Inventory: application to approved school boys. Joy Mott. 1969. iv + 27pp. (11 340063 2).

Home Office Research Studies (HORS)

1. *Workloads in children's departments. Eleanor Grey. 1969. vi + 75pp. (11 340101 9).

2. *Probationers in their social environment. A study of male probationers aged 17–20, together with an analysis of those reconvicted within twelve months. Martin Davies. 1969. vii + 204pp. (11 340102 7).

3. *Murder 1957 to 1968. A Home Office Statistical Division report on murder in England and Wales. Evelyn Gibson and S. Klein (with annex by the Scottish Home and Health Department on murder in Scotland). 1969. vi + 94pp. (11 340103 5).

4. Firearms in crime. A Home Office Statistical Division report on indictable offences involving firearms in England and Wales. A. D. Weatherhead and B. M. Robinson. 1970. viii + 39pp. (11 340104 3).

5. *Financial penalties and probation. Martin Davis. 1970. vi + 39pp. (11 3240105 1).

---

*Out of print

6. †Hostels for probationers. A study of the aims, working and variations in effectiveness of male probation hostels with special reference to the influence of the environment on delinquency. Ian Sinclair. 1971. ix + 200pp. (11 340106 X).

7. *Prediction methods in criminology — including a prediction study of young men on probation. Frances H. Simon. 1971. xi + 234pp. (11 340107 8).

8. *Study of the juvenile liaison scheme in West Ham 1961–65. Marilyn Taylor. 1971. vi + 46pp. (11 340108 6).

9. *Exploration in after-care, 1—After-care units in London, Liverpool and Manchester. Martin Silberman (Royal London Prisoners' Aid Society) and Brenda Chapman. II—After-care hostels receiving a Home Office grant. Ian Sinclair and David Snow (HORU). III—St. Martin of Tours House, Ayreh Leissner (National Bureau for Co-operation in Child Care). 1971. xi + 140pp. (11 340109 4).

10. A survey of adoption in Great Britain. Eleanor Grey in collaboration with Ronald M. Blunden. 1971. ix + 168pp. (11 340110 8).

11. *Thirteen-year-old approved school boys in 1962. Elizabeth Field, W. H. Hammond and J. Tizard. 1971. ix + 46pp. (11 34011 6).

12. Absconding from approved schools. R. G. V. Clarke and D. N. Martin. 1971. vi + 146pp. (11 340112 4).

13. An experiment in personality assessment of young men remanded in custody. H. Sylvia Anthony. 1972. viii + 79pp. (11 340113 2).

14. *Girl offenders aged 17–20 years. I—Statistics relating to girl offenders aged 17–20 years from 1960 to 1970. II—Re-offending by girls released from borstal or detention centre training. III—The problems of girls released from borstal training during their period on after-care. Jean Davies and Nancy Goodman. 1972. v + 77p. (11 340114 0).

15. *The controlled trial in institutional research—paradigm or pitfall for penal evaluators? R. V. G. Clarke and D. B. Cornish. 1972. v + 33pp. (11 340115 9).

16. *A survey of fine enforcement. Paul Softley. 1973. v + 65pp. (11 340116 7).

17. *An index of social environment—designed for use in social work research. Martin Davis. 1973. vi. + 63pp. (11 340117 5).

18. *Social enquiry reports and the probation service. Martin Davis and Andrea Knopf. 1973. v + 49pp. (11 340118 3).

19. *Depression, psychopathic personality and attempted suicide in a borstal sample. H. Sylvia Anthony. 1973. viii + 44pp. (0 11 340119 1).

20. *The use of bail and custody by London magistrates' courts before and after the Criminal Justice Act 1967. Frances Simon and Mollie Weatheritt. 1974. vi + 78pp. (0 11 340120 5).

21. *Social work in the environment. A study of one aspect of the probation practice. Martin Davis, with Margaret Rayfield, Alaster Calder and Tony Fowles. 1974. ix + 151pp. (0 11 340121 3).

22. Social work in prison. An experiment in the use of extended contact with offenders. Margaret Shaw, vii + 154pp. (0 11 340122 1).

23. Delinquency amongst opiate users. Joy Mott and Marilyn Taylor. vi + 31pp. (01 340663 0).

24. IMPACT. Intensive matched probation and after-care treatment. Vol. 1—The design of the probation experiment and an interim evaluation. M. S. Folkard, A. J. Fowles, B. C. McWilliams, W. McWilliams, D. D. Smith, D. E. Smith and G. R. Walmsey. 1974. v + 54pp. (0 11 340664 9).

25. The approved school experience. An account of boys' experiences of training under differing regimes of approved schools, with an attempt to evaluate the effectiveness of that training. Anne B. Dunlop. 1974. vii + 124pp. (0 11 340665 7).

26. *Absconding from open prisons. Charlotte Banks, Patricia Mayhew and R. J. Sapsford. 1975. viii + 89pp. (0 11 340666 5).

27. Driving while disqualified. Sue Kriefman. 1975. vi + 136pp. (0 11 340667 3).

28. Some male offenders' problems. I—Homeless offenders in Liverpool. W. McWilliams. II—Casework with short-term prisoners. Julie Holborn. 1975. x + 147pp. (011 340668 1).

29. *Community service orders. K. Pease, P. Durkin, I. Earnshaw, D. Payne and J. Thorpe. 1975. viii + 80pp. (0 11 340669 X).

*Out of print

30. Field Wing Bail Hostel: the first nine months. Frances Simon and Sheena Wilson. 1975. viii + 55pp. (0 11 340670 3).

31. Homicide in England and Wales 1967–1971. Evelyn Gibson. 1975. iv + 59pp. (0 11 340753 X).

32. Residential treatment and its effects on delinquency. D. B. Cornish and R. V. G. Clarke. 1975. vi + 74pp. (0 11 340672 X).

33. Further studies of female offenders. Part A: Borstal girls eight years after release. Nancy Goodman, Elizabeth Maloney and Jean Davies. Part B: The sentencing of women at the London Higher Courts. Nancy Goodman, Paul Durkin and Janet Halton. Part C: Girls appearing before a juvenile court. Jean Davies. 1976. vi + 114pp. (0 11 340673 8).

34. *Crime as opportunity. P. Mayhew, R. V. G. Clarke, A. Sturman and J. M. Hough. 1976. vii + 36pp. (0 11 340674 6).

35. The effectiveness of sentencing: a review of the literature. S. R. Brody. 1976. v + 89pp. (0 11 340675 4).

36. IMPACT. Intensive matched probation and after-care treatment. Vol II—The results of the experiment. M. S. Folkard, D. E. Smith and D. D. Smith. 1976 xi + 400pp. (0 11 340676 2).

37. Police cautioning in England and Wales. J. A. Ditchfield. 1976. v + 31pp. (0 11 340677 2).

38. Parole in England and Wales. C. P. Nuttall, with E. E. Barnard, A. J. Fowles, A. Frost, W. H. Hammond, P. Mayhew, K. Pease, R. Tarling and M. J. Weatheritt. 1977. vi + 90pp. (0 11 340678 9).

39. Community service assessed in 1976. K. Pease, S. Billingham and I. Earnshaw. 1977. vi + 29pp. (0 11 340679 7).

40. Screen violence and film censorship: a review of research. Stephen Brody. 1977. vii + 179pp. (0 11 340680 0).

41. Absconding from borstals. Gloria K. Laycock. 1977. v + 82pp. (0 11 340681 9).

42. Gambling: a review of the literature and its implications for policy and research. D. B. Cornish. 1978. xii + 284pp. (0 11 340682 7).

43. Compensation orders in magistrates' courts. Paul Softley. 1978. v + 41pp. (0 11 340683 5).

44. Research in criminal justice. John Croft. 1978. iv + 16pp. (0 11 340684 3).

45. Prison welfare: an account of an experiment at Liverpool. A. J. Fowles. 1978. v + 34pp. (0 11 340685 1).

46. Fines in magistrates' courts. Paul Softley. 1978. v + 42pp. (0 11 340686 X).

47. Tackling vandalism. R. V. G. Clarke (editor), F. J. Gladstone, A. Sturman and Sheena Wilson (contributors). 1978. vi + 91pp. (0 11 340687 8).

48. Social inquiry reports: a survey. Jennifer Thorpe. 1979. vi + 55pp. (0 11 340688 6).

49. Crime in public view. P. Mayhew, R. V. G. Clarke, J. N. Burrows, J. M. Hough and S. W. C. Winchester. 1979. v + 36pp. (0 11 340689 4).

50. *Crime and the community. John Croft. 1979. v + 16pp. (0 11 340690 8).

51. Life-sentence prisoners. David Smith (editor), Christopher Brown, Joan Worth, Roger Sapsford and Charlotte Banks (contributors). 1979. vi + 51pp. (0 11 340691 6).

52. Hostels for offenders. Jane E. Andrews, with an appendix by Bill Sheppard. 1979. v + 30pp. (0 11 340692 4).

53. Previous convictions, sentence and reconviction: a statistical study of a sample of 5,000 offenders convicted in January 1971. G. J. G. Phillpotts and L. B. Lancucki. 1979. v + 55p. (0 11 340693 2).

54. Sexual offences, consent and sentencing. Roy Walmsey and Karen White. 1979. vi + 77pp. (0 11 340694 0).

55. Crime prevention and the police. John Burrows, Paul Ekblom and Kevin Heal. 1979. v + 37pp. (0 11 340695 9).

56. Sentencing practice in magistrates' courts. Roger Tarling, with the assistance of Mollie Weatheritt. 1979. vii + 54pp. (0 11 340696).

57. Crime and comparative research. John Croft. 1979. vi + 16pp. (0 11 340697 5).

58. Race, crime and arrests. Philip Stevens and Carole F. Willis. 1979. v + 69pp. (0 11 340698 3).

---

*Out of print

59. Research and criminal policy. John Croft. 1980. iv + 14pp. (0 11 340699 1).

60. Junior attendance centres. Anne B. Dunlop. 1980. v + 47pp. (0 11 340700 9).

61. Police interrogation: an observational study in four police stations. Paul Softley, with the assistance of David Brown, Bob Forde, George Mair and David Moxon. 1980. vii+ 67pp. (0 11 340701 7).

62. Co-ordinating crime prevention efforts. F. J. Gladstone. 1980. v + 74pp. (0 11 340702 5).

63. Crime prevention publicity: an assessment. D. Riley and P. Mayhew. 1980. v + 47pp. (0 11 340703 3).

64. Taking offenders out of circulation. Stephen Brody and Roger Tarling. 1980. v + 46pp. (0 11 340704 1).

65. *Alcoholism and social policy: are we on the right lines? Mary Tuck. 1980. v + 30pp. (0 11 340705 X).

66. Persistent petty offenders. Suzan Fairhead. 1981. vi + 78pp. (0 11 340706 8).

67. Crime control and the police. Pauline Morris and Kevin Heal. 1981. v + 71pp. (0 11 340707 6).

68. Ethnic minorities in Britain: a study of trends in their positions since 1961. Simon Field, George Mair, Tom Rees and Philip Stevens. 1981. v + 48pp. (0 11 340708 4).

69. Managing criminological research. John Croft. 1981. iv + 17pp. (0 11 340709 2).

70. Ethnic minorities, crime and policing: a survey of the experiences of West Indians and whites. Mary Tuck and Peter Southgate. 1981 vi 50pp. (0 11 3240765 3).

71. Contested trials in magistrates' courts. Julie Vennard. 1982. v + 32pp. (0 11 340766 1).

72. Public disorder: a review of research and a study in one inner city area. Simon Field and Peter Southgate. 1982. v + 77pp. (0 11 340767 X).

73. Clearing up crime. John Burrows and Roger Tarling. 1982. vii + 31pp. (0 11 340768 8).

74. Residential burglary: the limits of prevention. Stuart Winchester and Hilary Jackson. 1982. v+ 47pp. (0 11 340769 6).

75. Concerning crime. John Croft. 1982. iv + 16pp. (0 11 340770 X).

76. The British Crime Survey: first report. Mike Hough and Pat Mayhew. 1983. v + 62pp. (0 11 340789 6).

77. Contacts between police and public: findings from the British Crime Survey. Peter Southgate and Paul Ekblom. 1984. v + 42pp. (0 11 340771 8).

78. Fear of crime in England and Wales. Michael Maxfield. 1984. v + 51pp. (0 11 340772 6).

79. Crime and police effectiveness. Ronald V. Clarke and Mike Hough. 1984. iv + 33pp. (0 11 340773 4).

80. The attitudes of ethnic minorities. Simon Field. 1984. v + 50pp. (0 11 340774 2).

81. Victims of crime: the dimensions of risk. Michael Gottfredson. 1984. v+ 54pp. (0 11 3240775 0).

82. The tape recording of police interviews with suspects: an interim report. Carole Willis. 1984. v+ 45pp. (0 11 340776 9).

83. Parental supervision and juvenile delinquency. David Riley and Margaret Shaw. 1985. v+ 90pp. (0 11 340799 8).

84. Adult prisons and prisoners in England and Wales 1970–82: a review of the findings of social research. Joy Mott. 1985. vi + 73pp. (0 11 340801 3).

85. Taking account of crime: key findings from the 1984 British Crime Survey. Mike Hough and Pat Mayhew. 1985. vi + 115pp. (0 11 340810 2).

86. Implementing crime prevention measures. Tim Hope. 1985. vi + 82pp. (0 11 340812 9).

87. Resettling refugees: the lessons of research. Simon Field. 1985. vi + 62pp. (0 11 340815 3).

88. Investigating Burglary: the measurement of police performance. John Burrows. 1986. v+ 36pp. (0 11 340824 2).

89. Personal violence. Roy Walmsey. 1986. vi + 87 pp. (0 11 340827 7).

---

*Out of print

ALSO

Designing out crime, R. V. G. Clarke and P. Mayhew (editors). 1980. vii + 186pp. (0 11 340732 7).

(This book collects, with an introduction, studies that were originally published in HORS 34, 47, 49, 55, 62 and 63 and which are illustrative of the 'situational' approach to crime prevention).

Policing today. Kevin Heal, Roger Tarling and John Burrows (editors). 1985. v + 181pp. (0 11 340800 5).

(This book brings together twelve separate studies on police matters during the last few years by the Unit. The collection records some relatively little known contributions to the debate on policing.)

The above HMSO publications can be purchased from Government Bookshops or through booksellers.

The following Home Officer research publications are available on request from the Home Officer Research and Planning Unit, 50 Queen Anne's Gate, London, SW1H 9AT.

Research Unit Papers (RUP)

1. Uniformed police work and management technology. J. M. Hough. 1980.

2. Supplementary information on sexual offences and sentencing. Roy Walmsley and Karen White. 1980.

3. Board of visitor adjudications. David Smith, Claire Austin and John Ditchfield. 1981.

4. Day centres and probations. Suzan Fairhead, with the assistance of J. Wilkinson-Grey. 1981.

Research and Planning Unit Papers (RPUP)

5. Ethnic minorities and complaints against the police. Philip Stevens and Carole Willis. 1982.

6. *Crime and public housing. Mike Hough and Pat Mayhew (editors). 1982.

7. *Abstracts of race relations research. George Mair and Philip Stevens (editors). 1982.

8. Police probationer training in race relations. Peter Southgate. 1982.

9. *The police response to calls from the public. Paul Ekblom and Kevin Heal. 1982.

10. City centre crime: a situational approach to prevention. Malcolm Ramsay. 1982.

11. Burglary in schools: the prospects for prevention. Tim Hope. 1982.

12. *Fine enforcement. Paul Softley and David Moxon. 1982.

13. Vietnamese refugees. Peter Jones. 1982.

14. Community resources for victims of crime. Karen Williams. 1983.

15. The use, effectiveness and impact of police stop and search powers. Carole Willis. 1983.

16. Acquittal rates. Sid Butler. 1983.

17. Criminal justice comparisons: the case of Scotland and England and Wales. Lorna J. F. Smith. 1983.

18. Time taken to deal with juveniles under criminal proceedings. Catherine Frankenburg and Roger Tarling.

19. Civilian review of complaints against the police: a survey of the United States literature. David C. Brown. 1983.

20. Police action on motoring offences. David Riley. 1983.

21. *Diverting drunks from the criminal justice system. Sue Kingsley and George Mair. 1983.

22. The staff resource implications of an independent prosecution system. Peter R. Jones. 1983.

23. Reducing the prison population: an explanatory study in Hampshire. David Smith, Bill Sheppard, George Mair and Karen Williams. 1984.

24. Criminal justice system model: magistrates' courts' sub-model. Susan Rice. 1984.

---

*Out of print.

25. Measures of police effectiveness and efficiency. Ian Sinclair and Clive Miller. 1984.

26. Punishment practice by prison Boards of Visitors. Susan Iles, Adrienne Connors, Chris May, Joy Mott, 1984.

27. *Reparation, conciliation and mediation. Tony Marshall. 1984.

28. Magistrates domestic courts: new perspectives. Tony Marshall (editor). 1984.

29. Racism awareness training for the police. Peter Southgate. 1984.

30. Community constables: a study of policing initiative. David Brown and Susan Iles. 1985.

31. Recruiting volunteers. Hilary Jackson. 1985.

32. Juvenile sentencing: is there a tariff? David Moxon, Peter Jones and Roger Tarling. 1985.

33. Bringing people together: mediation and reparation projects in Great Britain. Tony Marshall and Martin Walpole. 1985.

34. Rewards in the absence of the accused. Chris May. 1985.

35. Modelling the criminal justice system. Patricia M. Morgan. 1986.

36. The criminal justice system model: the flow model. Hugh Pullinger. 1986.

37. Burglary: police actions and victim views. John Burrows. 1986.

Research Bulletin
The Research Bulletin is published twice a year and consists mainly of short articles relating to projects which are part of the Home Office Research and Planning Unit's research programme.

---

*Out of print.

Printed for Her Majesty's Stationery Office by Robendene Ltd., Amersham.
Dd 739344 C13 5/86